EMOTION AND MOTIVATION

Longman Essential Psychology
Series editor: Andrew M. Colman

Other titles in this series:

Abnormal Psychology
Arnold A. Lazarus and Andrew M. Colman

Applications of Psychology
Andrew M. Colman

Biological Aspects of Behaviour
Daniel Kimble and Andrew M. Colman

Cognitive Psychology
Christopher C. French and Andrew M. Colman

Controversies in Psychology
Andrew M. Colman

Developmental Psychology
Peter E. Bryant and Andrew M. Colman

Individual Differences and Personality
Sarah E. Hampson and Andrew M. Colman

Learning and Skills
Nicholas J. Mackintosh and Andrew M. Colman

Psychological Research Methods and Statistics
Andrew M. Colman

Sensation and Perception
Richard L. Gregory and Andrew M. Colman

Social Psychology
Michael Argyle and Andrew M. Colman

EMOTION AND MOTIVATION

EDITED BY

Brian Parkinson
and
Andrew M. Colman

LONGMAN
London and New York

Longman Group Limited
Longman House, Burnt Mill
Harlow, Essex CM20 2JE, England
and Associated Companies throughout the world.

Published in the United States of America
by Longman Publishing, New York

© 1994 Routledge
This edition © 1995 Longman Group Limited
Compilation © 1995 Andrew Colman

This edition first published 1995

ISBN 0 582 27808 2 PPR

British Library Cataloguing-in-Publication Data
A catalogue record for this book is available from the British Library.

Library of Congress Cataloging-in-Publication Data
A catalogue record for this book is available from the Library of Congress.

Typeset by 25 in 10/12pt Times
Printed and bound by Bookcraft (Bath) Ltd

CONTENTS

NOTES ON EDITORS AND CONTRIBUTORS

JOHN BANCROFT qualified in medicine from Cambridge University and St George's Hospital, London, and completed psychiatric training at the Maudsley Hospital, London. He was Clinical Reader in Psychiatry at Oxford University before joining the Medical Research Council Reproductive Biology Unit in Edinburgh in 1976. He has been involved in research into human sexuality and the clinical management of its problems for most of his career. His current research interest is the relationship between reproductive hormones and the well-being and sexuality of women. He is the author of *Human Sexuality and its Problems* (2nd edn, 1989).

JOHN E. BLUNDELL studied for his doctorate at the Institute of Neurology, University of London. He is the director of a research group at Leeds University specializing in the control of human appetite with particular reference to the relationships among nutrition, physiology, and behaviour. He is the author of a science citation classic on the role of the neurotransmitter serotonin in appetite control entitled "Is there a role for Serotonin (5-hydroxytryptamine) in feeding?" (*International Journal of Obesity*, 1977, *1*, 15–42) and has been awarded the 25th International Prize in Modern Nutrition (1992).

ANDREW M. COLMAN is Reader in Psychology at the University of Leicester, having previously taught at Rhodes and Cape Town Universities in South Africa. He is the founder and former editor of the journal *Current Psychology* and Chief Examiner for the British Psychological Society's Qualifying Examination. His books include *Facts, Fallacies and Frauds in Psychology* (1987), *What is Psychology? The Inside Story* (2nd edn, 1988), and *Game Theory and its Applications in the Social and Biological Sciences* (2nd edn, 1995).

ROBERT J. GATCHEL is Professor of Psychiatry and Rehabilitation Science at the University of Texas Southwestern Medical Center at Dallas. He received his BA from the State University of New York at Stony Brook, and his PhD in clinical psychology from the University of Wisconsin. He has conducted extensive research on psychophysiological concomitants of stress and emotion, clinical applications of biofeedback and self-regulation techniques, and the assessment and treatment of chronic low back pain disability. He is on the editorial board of numerous journals, and is a fellow of the American Psychological Association and the Academy of Behavioral Medicine Research, as well as various other professional societies. He is the author of over 100 scientific publications and chapters, and has authored or edited 10 books, including (as co-author with A. Baum and D. S. Krantz) *An Introduction to Health Psychology* (1989).

RUSSELL G. GEEN is Curators' Professor of Psychology at the University of Missouri, Columbia. A graduate of the University of Wisconsin (PhD, 1967), he was editor of the *Journal of Research in Personality* from 1977 to 1988 and became editor of the *Journal of Personality and Social Psychology: Personality Processes and Individual Differences* in 1991. He has published five books, including (as co-author with W. Beatty and R. M. Arkin) *Human Motivation* (1984) and is the author of *Human Aggression* (1990).

ANDREW J. HILL is Senior Lecturer in Behavioural Sciences at Leeds University Medical School. His doctorate was on hunger motivation and he has published extensively on this issue. Other research interests include the psychology of food cravings, and the emergence of dieting and weight control during childhood and adolescence.

BRIAN PARKINSON studied psychology as an undergraduate and postgraduate at Manchester University, where he received his PhD in 1983. He is currently Lecturer in Psychology at the University of Leicester. His interests concern the interrelations between the everyday use of emotional concepts and more formal psychological theories of emotion. His most recent research concerns role-prescribed emotion in the workplace and strategies of expressive management among high-contact service employees.

SERIES EDITOR'S PREFACE

The *Longman Essential Psychology* series comprises twelve concise and inexpensive paperback volumes covering all of the major topics studied in undergraduate psychology degree courses. The series is intended chiefly for students of psychology and other subjects with psychology components, including medicine, nursing, sociology, social work, and education. Each volume contains five or six accessibly written chapters by acknowledged authorities in their fields, and each chapter includes a list of references and a small number of recommendations for further reading.

Most of the material was prepared originally for the Routledge *Companion Encyclopedia of Psychology* but with a view to later paperback subdivision − the contributors were asked to keep future textbook readers at the front of their minds. Additional material has been added for the paperback series: new co-editors have been recruited for nine of the volumes that deal with highly specialized topics, and each volume has a new introduction, a glossary of technical terms including a number of entries written specially for this edition, and a comprehensive new index.

I am grateful to my literary agents Sheila Watson and Amanda Little for clearing a path through difficult terrain towards the publication of this series, to Sarah Caro of Longman for her patient and efficient preparation of the series, to Brian Parkinson, David Stretch, and Susan Dye for useful advice and comments, and to Carolyn Preston for helping with the compilation of the glossaries.

ANDREW M. COLMAN

INTRODUCTION

Brian Parkinson and Andrew M. Colman
University of Leicester, England

Among the many possible ways of classifying human mental functions, one of the most widely accepted (for example, Hilgard, 1980) defines three separate areas of cognition (thinking), affect (feeling), and conation (willing). Emotion is one of the most important and thoroughly explored forms of affect, and motivation is essentially just a new name for conation, therefore this volume might be seen, from one angle at least, as spanning almost two thirds of psychology. According to a simpler classification, the two basic operations of the mind relate to knowledge and desire, and emotion and motivation both belong mainly in the latter category. In many ways, this two-way classification reflects more accurately how contemporary psychology draws its boundaries, with cognition on one side and whatever cognition excludes, including emotion and motivation, on the other, almost by default.

What do emotion and motivation have in common? Both load high on intensity or energy rather than direction or information in the terms of Duffy's (1962) interpretation of the knowledge–desire dichotomy. Intuitively, both seem characterized by heat and pressure (cf. Kövecses, 1990) in contrast to the apparent coldness of cognition. Both move us in some way, as implied by the common Latin root of both words (*movere*, to move). But these metaphors do not get us very far with a scientific understanding of the phenomena in question; more important are the underlying processes.

Emotion and motivation both depend on the relationship between the organism and its environment. In the case of emotion, the emphasis is on the evaluative aspect of this relationship: how the situation makes the person feel; in the case of motivation, it is how the individual acts with respect to the situation that is of interest (Kuhl, 1986). There are obvious links between emotion and motivation, because situational evaluations largely determine action priorities: liking implies affinity or attraction and disliking repulsion. In other words, emotions are often precursors of motivational phenomena; they signal our inclinations to act in particular ways towards specified portions of the environment (see, for example, Oatley, 1992).

Correspondingly, if our efforts lead us to attain an intended goal we tend to evaluate this outcome positively, and if our actions are thwarted the resulting emotion tends to be negative (cf. Carver & Scheier, 1990). Emotions may thus serve partly as rewards or punishments for motivated behaviour. Much of human activity may in fact be driven by affect-regulatory goals of one form or another: we often do things because we anticipate that they will make us feel better in some way (for example, Thayer, Newman & McClain, 1994). Furthermore, having performed an action that results in pleasant affective consequences, we are more likely to behave similarly in the future, according to simple principles of reinforcement. But hedonism of this kind cannot account for all varieties of motivational phenomena, because it is apparent that we also strive towards more abstract ends such as mastery or understanding. Although some theorists believe that the pleasure principle is indirectly at work even in these cases, satisfaction is sometimes deferred almost indefinitely.

Motivation encompasses a range of interlocking processes, including biologically defined urges and desires, acquired affinities and aversions, and the implementation of conscious intentions. A complete explanation of any motivational phenomenon always includes reference to an interaction of both internal and external factors, and to instinct as well as learning, although obviously different factors may be relatively more important in different cases.

This book covers a variety of motivational phenomena including many that relate specifically to emotion and emotion-regulation. In each case, the contributions of both biological and social variables and the interrelation of environmental and personal factors is considered. Although the diversity of processes associated with motivation and emotion is too great to permit any simple overarching explanatory framework, enough representative examples are included here to provide a general picture of these phenomena.

Brian Parkinson's chapter 1 gives a general background to the psychology of emotion. The concept is introduced by cataloguing examples of emotions (love, anger, fear, and so on), by exploring the internal constitution of emotional reactions, and finally by contrasting emotion with cognition. Emotion is conceived as a syndrome of more or less integrated components usually including the following four factors: cognitive appraisals, bodily reactions, action tendencies, and expressive movements.

The component closest to the core of the emotional syndrome is appraisal – the process whereby the personal significance of the current encounter with the environment is interpreted and evaluated (for example, Smith &

Lazarus, 1993). Appraisal largely determines the quality and intensity of experienced emotion and carries direct implications for motivation. For example, if you appraise a situation as one in which something untoward has occurred as a consequence of someone else's action or neglect, and if this outcome is of sufficient importance to you, then the immediate result is likely to be the emotion of anger. Being angry usually involves a felt urge to hit out at the perpetrator either literally or metaphorically, which may be expressed by baring the teeth and adopting a forward-leaning posture. This state of action readiness (Frijda, 1986) may also be manifested in preparatory physiological adjustments designed mainly to mobilize metabolic energy; thus appraisal of personal concerns leads inexorably to motivational tendencies.

To the extent that appraisal is a cognitive process, the account just offered suggests that emotions are closely related to cognitions. However, from an intuitive point of view and in terms of the trichotomy of mental operations mentioned above, these two faculties are quite separate. This paradox arises because, although the experiences of feeling and thinking are obviously distinct, the psychological processes underlying them are continually interacting, in much the same way as emotional and motivational mechanisms are often hard to untangle in ongoing encounters.

Chapter 2 by John E. Blundell and Andrew J. Hill deals with hunger, the feeling associated with a desire for food, and appetite, the basic motivation underlying eating. Although eating is essential for biological survival, this chapter shows how even here complex interactions between organismic and environmental variables control the relevant responses. For example, although humans are apparently equipped with physiological mechanisms that automatically regulate food intake so that it matches ongoing energy requirements, during dieting deliberate intentional control of eating may to some extent overrule these lower homeostatic processes. Furthermore, eating depends on the amount and variety of food easily available in the environment.

The relationship between hunger and eating is a particular instance of the general relationship between affect and behaviour. Hunger provides signals that inform the person that eating is necessary, much as emotional states signal the need for relevant action. The extent of these signals depends not only on direct registration of the need for food but also on cultural conventions about the frequency and timing of eating episodes and on external stimuli that activate relevant sensations.

Of course, eating may be motivated by factors other than hunger. For example, many people claim that food serves a comfort function and helps to alleviate unpleasant emotions. At other times eating or not eating may be motivated by apparently non-emotional factors, as illustrated by the phenomena of competitive binges and religious fasting ceremonies. A range of cultural practices have developed around food consumption which take the phenomenon beyond the realm of simple sustenance goals. Clearly, the motivations underlying even a basic biological behaviour like eating do not depend simply on self-correcting pre-wired processes.

The topic of chapter 3 by Russell G. Geen is social motivation, which relates to the various processes whereby the presence of other people affects performance on achievement-related tasks. Research suggests that people's performance when under the scrutiny of others tends to be improved in the case of easy tasks (social facilitation) but impaired in the case of difficult tasks (social inhibition). Geen considers a range of possible explanations for these effects, most of which depend on the basic idea that audiences tend to activate a motivational state that has different effects on different kinds of activity. For example, observation by other people may make us anxious about the impression we are likely to create should we visibly fail (evaluation apprehension). Our consequent emotional condition may make us distracted, increase our motivation to succeed, evoke higher achievement standards, enhance self-awareness, and so on, and any of these factors might improve or hinder our performance.

In general, the mere presence of other people tends to increase the potential emotional costs of failure and to enhance the emotional benefits of success. In an interpersonal situation, we are subject to the rewards and punishments deriving directly from performance outcomes and we must also be prepared to take the consequences of the audience's reactions to our success or failure. Similarly, if others are performing the same task, they may do better or worse than us, making our own performance seem relatively better or worse by comparison. Thus, both actual and anticipated emotion may play a part in the unfolding of the social motivational drama.

In chapter 4, John Bancroft discusses the motives and mechanisms underlying sexual behaviour. As in the case of eating, the appetite for sex depends on social and emotional considerations in addition to basic physiological processes. For example, we may engage in sexual activity to reduce anxiety, to assert our masculinity or femininity, or simply for monetary payment, as well as for reasons of physical pleasure or because we are somehow biologically programmed to reproduce. Correspondingly, sexual feelings have obvious neurochemical underpinnings but are also crucially dependent on individual cognitive interpretations and culturally derived understandings about acceptable modes of interaction. In adult humans, sexual contact often occurs within more or less stable relationships, and rules of engagement are explicitly or implicitly negotiated between participants against a backdrop of societal conventions.

Emotion is implicated in the sexual process in a number of ways. Having sex may be a means of expressing feelings towards a partner as well as a way of deriving emotional satisfaction. Also, it is generally believed that certain emotional states such as depression lessen the sexual drive, while other affective conditions such as amusement may facilitate sexual response.

In the final chapter of the book, Robert J. Gatchel provides an overview of theory and research on stress and coping. Stress is usually viewed as a psychobiological phenomenon whereby an appraisal that situational demands exceed available resources triggers a generalized physiological alarm response, which may itself cause damage to the organism if it persists. Thus, psychologically unpleasant situations are thought to activate systems that are biologically designed to withstand acute physical threats. Of course, the feelings of pressure or strain that we often report when overworked do not necessarily imply this kind of direct physiological involvement and may not in themselves threaten our health. However, the emotions associated with stressful episodes may lead us to neglect our well-being by eating badly or drinking too much, for example.

Gatchel's chapter discusses the variety of situational factors that lead to stress, ranging from everyday hassles, through major life events, to more cataclysmic outcomes affecting large groups of people simultaneously. Clearly, the nature of the stressor is likely to determine the degree and quality of its impact. Correspondingly, different stressors tend to evoke different types of responses. For example, coping processes are believed to vary according to whether the situation is perceived as controllable or uncontrollable. When it is controllable, direct action designed specifically to correct the stressful aspects of the situation (problem-focused coping) is more appropriate, whereas when it is uncontrollable, people may be able only to work on their affective reactions to what has happened and try to make themselves feel better about it (emotion-focused coping). The emotion-focused coping process is a good example of a motivational phenomenon that is specifically directed at affect regulation and is usually determined by relatively high-level psychological processes based on intentionality and deliberation.

The main emphasis of most current accounts of stress phenomena is on how reappraisal and individual coping (sometimes supplemented by social support) can ameliorate the negative effects of environmental demands. However, it should be remembered that some forms of situational constraint cannot simply be wished away or easily dealt with by personal action. Many people in contemporary society lack psychological room for manoeuvre and are caught within institutional traps from which there is no obvious escape route.

We hope that the brief tour of emotion and motivation provided in this book directs readers to many of the important landmarks of research in this area. Of course, there is also ground that we have not been able to cover (see Weiner, 1992, for a more extensive account of motivation; Parkinson, 1995, or Plutchik, 1994, for a more detailed analysis of emotion; and the suggestions for further reading at the end of each of the chapters for more information on the specific topics covered). No general model of motivational effects is offered here, whether based on cybernetic principles (for example, Carver & Scheier, 1990) or on hierarchies of needs (for example, Maslow, 1962). Furthermore, there is little emphasis in this book on the motivations underlying actions that unfold in the long term as part of life plans shaped by developing high-level values or self-actualization goals. These omissions arise mainly because much of the relevant scientific work remains to be done. It is therefore to be hoped that future psychological research will develop some of the ideas presented here to incorporate a broader range of topics and push towards a more integrated analysis of the field.

The contents of this book leads us to reject the simplistic three-way division of psychology sketched out above. Any comprehensive account of motivational or emotional processes implies complex interactions between a range of factors, many of which are likely to involve cognition at some level. Part of the importance of the subject area of motivation and emotion, however, is that the phenomena in question remind us that a psychology based solely on information-processing concepts will always fail to tell the whole story.

REFERENCES

Carver, C. S., & Scheier, M. F. (1990). Origins and functions of positive and negative affect: A control-process view. *Psychological Review*, *97*, 19–35.

Duffy, E. (1962). *Activation and behavior*. New York: Wiley.

Frijda, N. H. (1986). *The emotions*. Cambridge: Cambridge University Press.

Hilgard, E. R. (1980). The trilogy of mind: Cognition, affection, and conation. *Journal of the History of the Behavioral Sciences*, *16*, 107–17.

Kövecses, Z. (1990). *Emotion concepts*. New York: Springer-Verlag.

Kuhl, J. (1986). Motivation and information processing: A new look at decision making, dynamic change, and action control. In R. M. Sorrentino & E. T. Higgins (eds), *Handbook of motivation and cognition: Foundations of social behavior*, Chichester: Wiley, pp. 404.

Maslow, A. H. (1962). *Toward a psychology of being*, Princeton, NJ: Van Nostrand.

Oatley, K. (1992). *Best laid schemes: The psychology of emotions*. Cambridge: Cambridge University Press.

Parkinson, B. (1995). *Ideas and realities of emotion*. London: Routledge.

Plutchik, R. (1994). *The psychology and biology of emotion*. New York: HarperCollins.

Smith, C. A., & Lazarus, R. S. (1993), Appraisal components, core relational themes, and the emotions. *Cognition and Emotion*, *7*, 233–69.

Thayer, R. E., Newman, J. R., & McClain, T. M. (1994). Self-regulation of mood: Strategies for changing a bad mood, raising energy, and reducing tension. *Journal of Personality and Social Psychology*, *64*, 910–25.

Weiner, B. (1992). *Human motivation: Metaphors, theories, and research*, New York: Sage.

EMOTION

Brian Parkinson

University of Leicester, England

It has often been remarked that everyone knows perfectly well what emotion is, but no one can define it. In fact, as with most paradoxes, this is not quite true. On the one hand, not everyone agrees about what emotion is. Although most people do seem to have their own intuitive understanding of the term, there is nevertheless some uncertainty about what counts as an emotion, and even how various different emotional conditions such as anger, embarrassment, pride and so on are manifested. People from different cultures and different eras sometimes have very different conceptions of emotions (e.g., Harré, 1986; Lutz, 1988) and their lists of individual states that come under the general heading may differ quite substantially.

On the other hand, there are at least some states, such as happiness and anger, that few people within western culture would disagree are emotional. Similarly, there is a degree of consensus about how to define the phenomenon in question. When we look at the kinds of things most people (including psychologists) want to call emotions, we can see that they share certain common features to a greater or lesser extent, and this certainly allows a provisional definition. But more of this in a moment.

Clearly, there are several ways of approaching the question of what emotion is, and this chapter covers some of these different angles. First, you can define emotion by giving examples of items that belong in the category, and of the conditions that clearly do not. The question of membership in the class of emotions seems more easily answerable for some states than for others. For example, is love an emotion? Is lust? Is shopping? I shall consider the idea that not all examples of emotions are equally good representatives of the category.

A second way of defining emotion is by looking at the different aspects and components of emotional experience, and I shall next follow this approach, concentrating on four important aspects of emotional experience: cognitive evaluations of the situation, bodily responses, facial (and other) expressions, and action impulses. I shall argue that emotions usually possess at least most of these characteristics but that, with the possible exception of the evaluative factor, none of them should be seen as defining or necessary features of emotional experience.

A third way of characterizing emotion is to consider how the various aspects combine with one another, and how they interact to make an emotional episode what it is. I shall look at the internal structure of emotional experience and review some of the alternative causal sequences that have been proposed by psychologists to explain how emotion happens.

Finally, emotion can be defined by relating and contrasting it with other psychological functions. I shall discuss the relationships and contrasts between emotion and cognition in order to clarify how emotion fits in with general psychological functioning.

By the end of the chapter, the reader should be in a better position to know how psychologists might answer the question "What is an emotion?" For now, I shall suggest a provisional definition based upon a common-sense understanding of the concept. What, then, do the states that people think of as emotional have in common with one another?

To make a start on this definition, I want to argue that emotions are characteristically *intentional* states. By this I mean that they take an object of some sort. It is hard to imagine a pure state of pride, anger, or love without the state being directed at something: you are proud of your success, angry with someone who has insulted you, in love with someone in particular, rather than just proud, angry, or in love per se (e.g., Averill, 1980). The apparent exceptions to this rule are states such as happiness, boredom, and depression, which may sometimes seem quite diffuse and unfocused. According to the definition I am suggesting, these conditions would not qualify as bona fide emotions (see below).

So, emotions imply a certain relationship between a person and some object, person (including the self), or event (real, remembered, or imagined).

My second assumption is that this relation is an intrinsically *evaluative* one. A defining feature of emotion seems to be that when emotional we feel good or bad, approving or disapproving, relieved or disappointed about some state of affairs. Third and finally, this evaluative attitude is not a permanent and enduring aspect of our way of relating to the world, but a disruption or break from our background position. Even the derivation of the word "emotion" suggests a *move away* from normal functioning, something that comes over us for a while. Thus, emotions are states that are more or less transient and short lived.

This preliminary definition also allows us to distinguish emotions from related states such as moods (cf. Clark & Isen, 1982). Like emotions, moods have an evaluative component and feel good or bad (i.e., they too are *affective* states); unlike emotions, moods do not usually take a definite object (you can just be grumpy as a result of "getting out of bed the wrong side" without any particular focus to the experience); unlike emotions, moods can persist for relatively long periods of time.

To summarize, although it is not easy to come up with a thoroughgoing definition of emotion that will include all the phenomena that non-psychologists might want to call emotion (and exclude all those that they would not), it is still true that certain characteristics are agreed to be fairly central defining features of emotion. The chances are, if someone is emotional, that person will have a positive or a negative felt reaction to some definite object (whether imagined or real), and this reaction will not last too long. In other words, I shall consider emotions to be evaluative, affective, intentional, and short-term conditions.

THE CATEGORY OF EMOTION

The simplest and most obvious way of explaining what emotion is, is by giving examples. It seems reasonable to assume that once we know what items are included in the category of emotion, we shall have a pretty good idea of what an emotion is. Unfortunately, the problem of defining emotion does not go away this easily because there is less than universal agreement about what conditions count as emotions. Psychologists as well as non-psychologists differ in their opinions of whether certain states are or are not emotional.

Nevertheless, there is some consensus concerning a few clear examples of emotion. Fehr and Russell (1984) asked Canadian college students to rate a series of emotion terms on the basis of how closely they represented the category. *Love* was rated as the best example of an emotion overall, followed by *hate, anger, sadness,* and *happiness.* These same words also tended to be the ones that most readily sprang to mind when the students were asked to list emotions (see Table 1).

Other words, such as *pride, hope, lust, pain,* and *hunger,* were rated as

Table 1 Two top tens of representative emotions

Common-sense chart	Psychologists' chart
Happiness (152)	Fear (9)
Anger (149)	Anger (7)
Sadness (136)	Disgust (6)
Love (124)	Sadness (5)
Fear (96)	Joy (5)
Hate (89)	Surprise (5)
Joy (82)	Rage (4)
Excitement (53)	Love (3)
Anxiety (50)	Happiness (3)
Depression (42)	Interest (3)

Source: Based on free listings of emotion names by 200 subjects (Fehr & Russell, 1984)

Source: Based on lists of "basic emotions" produced by 14 representative basic emotions theorists (Ortony & Turner, 1991)

Note: Numbers in parentheses reflect number of selections of the emotion names by informants

relatively poorer examples of emotions. Some people thought that these conditions were emotional and some did not. Fehr and Russell concluded that the category of emotion is not one around which any sharp dividing line can be drawn, separating emotions on the inside from other, non-emotional states on the outside. Rather, there are many states that might be labelled as emotions in some circumstances but not others, and by certain people but not everyone. The class of emotional phenomena, in such a view, is bounded by fuzzy rather than distinct edges.

This approach to the structure of categories is known as the *prototype approach* (Rosch, 1978), because the category is considered to be defined by its most central and characteristic example or prototype. Membership of the category then depends upon degree of similarity to this prototype: the closer resemblance a particular item shows to the prototype, the more likely it is to be included in the category, but all-or-none judgements are often difficult. The alternative *classical* view of categories is that it is possible to draw up a list of defining features that allow us to determine exactly what belongs inside a category and what belongs outside. Some concepts have very tight and precise definitions which allow us to make incontestable decisions about what counts as a member of the category and what doesn't. For example, a square *is* a quadrilateral with sides of equal length and vertices of 90 degrees. Given my earlier comments about the difficulty of defining emotion in a precise manner, it will be no surprise that I see problems with a classical approach to the category, the most obvious one being that there are few characteristics that all emotions have in common, but other non-emotional states do not also share (but see Clore & Ortony, 1991, for an alternative point of view).

When psychologists have drawn up their own lists of emotions, they too have often disagreed with one another. Some theorists have suggested that there is a small set of primary emotions, based on the genetic inheritance of the species or the commonalities in human development (see Table 1). For example, Ekman and Friesen (1971) suggested that there are six basic biologically programmed emotions: *happiness*, *sadness*, *fear*, *anger*, *surprise*, and *disgust*, each with its own distinctive facial expression. In the primary emotion view, other non-primary emotions are thought to be blends of the basic ones. However, the fact that psychologists have disagreed about which emotions are basic (and about whether states such as surprise are even emotions, let alone basic emotions) tends to undermine the credibility of the view that certain states are basically, irreducibly, and inescapably emotional. Indeed, some psychologists have denied that there is any good reason to suppose that there are *basic* emotions at all (Ortony & Turner, 1991).

Having considered the various examples of emotion, there still remains the question of how these examples themselves should be defined. Like the concept of emotion in general, particular emotional terms also seem to have prototypical rather than classical definitions. For example, saying that someone is angry implies a variety of claims about that person's experience, expression, and likely behaviour, but not all of these need apply for anger to be a valid description of the state. Next I shall look at the different components of emotion, before considering the ways in which these aspects are interrelated and build the complete experience of an emotional state.

COMPONENTS OF EMOTION

Psychological research into emotion has focused on four variables that are associated with emotional experience. I shall consider each of these factors in turn as characteristics of emotional experience. The four kinds of phenomena are the following: situational evaluations, bodily changes, expressive behaviours, and motivated actions. For example, an angry person will typically evaluate the situation in terms of some kind of insult against himself or herself, will experience physical symptoms such as a quickened heartbeat and flushing of the face, will show a characteristic facial expression with clenched teeth and a knitted brow, and will have the impulse to hit out at the antagonist in some literal or metaphorical way. This represents the prototype of our category of anger. Real-life examples of anger may share a large proportion of these features but usually not all of them. Although it is hard to conceive of someone being angry without evaluating the situation in terms of a personal slight, none of the other aspects of the emotion are necessary to anger.

Situational evaluations and interpretations

Above, I suggested that emotional states typically involve an evaluative relationship between the person and an intentional object. This evaluative aspect appears to be quite central to what we mean by emotion. Unless we are experiencing the situation as positive or negative, in a good or a bad light, it seems to make little sense to claim that we are emotional.

Arnold (1960) emphasized the importance of the evaluative aspect of emotion with her concept of *appraisal*, which refers to the process whereby the personal relevance of the emotional object is apprehended: "To arouse an emotion, the object must be appraised as affecting me in some way, affecting me personally as an individual with my particular experience and my particular aims" (p. 171).

Lazarus (1968) suggested that emotional appraisal has two facets, which he called *primary appraisal* and *secondary appraisal*. In primary appraisal, the individual evaluates the relevance of the current situation to personal well-being, weighing up whether it has good or bad implications for prevailing concerns, and implicitly asking the question: "Am I in trouble or am I OK?" In secondary appraisal, the individual evaluates his or her capacity for dealing with the situation (coping potential), asking, in other words, "What can be done about it?"

Clearly, different emotions are characterized by different evaluations of the situation. For example, positive emotions such as happiness and pride are associated with primary appraisals that the situation is beneficial to personal concerns, whereas negative emotions such as anger, fear, and sadness suggest that the situation is being appraised as detrimental to the individual. Emotions may be further differentiated on the basis of aspects of secondary appraisal: for example, if the situation is appraised as unfavourable, and coping potential is appraised as low and unlikely to improve, then the emotional state experienced is likely to be depression or sadness. On the other hand, if the situation is appraised as unfavourable but coping potential is appraised as high, then the emotion is more likely to be felt as hope (Smith & Lazarus, 1990).

Several studies have investigated the different appraisals that are associated with different emotions. For example, Smith and Ellsworth (1985) asked students to think of occasions in the past when they had experienced fifteen specific emotional states such as pride, anger, and so on. The students then answered various questions about their evaluations of these remembered situations, using a series of rating scales. Smith and Ellsworth found that characteristic patterns of ratings were associated with the different emotions. Other experiments (e.g., Frijda, Kuipers, & ter Schure, 1989) have produced broadly consistent findings.

From this research it can be concluded that a wide variety of emotional experiences can be differentiated using a relatively small set of appraisal dimensions. The most important dimensions relate to the event's pleasantness or unpleasantness; its unfamiliarity or familiarity; its unexpectedness; its beneficial or harmful implications; uncertainty about its implications; your own and other people's responsibility for the event; the controllability or uncontrollability of the event; whether the event is relevant to your well-being or someone else's; and whether the event conforms to or conflicts with your norms. The evidence suggests that these dimensions are differentially *symptomatic* of the different emotions. I shall return to the separate issue of whether they also play a *causal* role in distinguishing emotions in a later section.

Bodily changes

Emotion has a strong intuitive connection with the heart and with the guts (Averill, 1974). Correspondingly, psychologists have been discussing and investigating the bodily accompaniments of emotional states since the 1880s, (e.g., James, 1884).

At the centre of this research is a long-standing controversy about whether distinctive patterns of physiological response accompany the various possible emotional states (Ekman, Levenson, & Friesen, 1983). Cannon (1929) argued that all the excited emotions such as anger and fear are actually accompanied by the same state: a generalized emergency response preparing the body for vigorous activity. This pattern, known as *sympathetic arousal*, is based on a diffuse activation of the sympathetic division of the autonomic nervous system and produces a general increase in metabolic rate and energy mobilization in the body. The following set of responses characteristically occur: increase in heart rate and blood pressure, increased respiratory volume, constriction of the blood vessels in the skin (pallor), dilation of pupils, arrest of gastro-intestinal activity, decreased salivation (dry mouth), and increased action of the sweat glands. The response system is partly mediated by increased adrenaline (epinephrine) secretion, which may also result in trembling, and feelings of cold.

Although there is little convincing scientific evidence that there are definite relationships between distinctive body states and different emotions, people still report different bodily symptoms associated with anger, fear, sadness, and so on (e.g., Nieuwenhuyse, Offenberg, & Frijda, 1987). There are a number of possible reasons for this. First, it may be that intense emotions actually do have distinctive bodily accompaniments, but the weaker reactions that are evoked in the laboratory (for practical and ethical reasons) are less clearly differentiated. In this case, subjects' beliefs about distinctive bodily accompaniments may still be correct. Second, it is possible that cultural stereotypes about what symptoms are supposed to be associated with different emotions distort people's interpretations of their own bodily responses (Rimé, Philippot, & Cisamolo, 1990). Finally, it may be that

7

different emotions focus awareness on different parts of the body because of their symbolic content; although the actual physiological response is diffuse, only the relevant symptoms are picked up by the person having the emotional experience. For example, although embarrassment may be accompanied by a wide variety of physiological responses, the fact that the emotion is concerned with feelings of exaggerated social visibility makes facial flushing the most salient symptom. The best conclusion that can be drawn from the research is that it is important to maintain a distinction between felt bodily symptoms of emotion, and the actual physiological changes that may or may not underlie them.

Emotional expression

One of the most obvious indices of emotional experience, precisely because we are socially attuned to it, is expressive behaviour. By expression, I mean movement and sounds made by someone indicating the presence of emotion to someone else. These movements and sounds may not be deliberate or intentional, but they will still be expressive to the extent that they communicate emotional information. The face is the most important channel of emotional expression, partly because it is capable of a wide variety of subtly patterned movements. In addition, emotion may be expressed through tone of voice, bodily posture, and gestures.

Since Darwin (1872), it has been commonly believed that at least some facial expressions are genetically programmed in humans. Evidence for this idea has come from studies that show that a small set of facial expressions are consistently identified by people coming from a large variety of cultures including some which have had little contact with westerners (Ekman & Friesen, 1971). For example, four facial expressions (anger, disgust, happiness, and sadness) posed by members of a pre-literate culture were recognized at better than chance level by American students. The evidence relating to other emotional expressions is less convincing. Furthermore, real-life emotional states are accompanied by continually changing facial expressions which are rarely as clearcut as those used in the studies mentioned.

Emotional meaning can also be conveyed by body posture, limb movements, and so on. In fact, facial expressions are often part of more general action patterns which include postural changes and integrated movements of the whole body. Finally, emotion may be expressed vocally, in speech intonation and pitch and so on (Scherer, 1986). Research evidence suggests that the emotional meaning of contentless speech is recognized about as well as that of facial expression.

Motivated action

The fourth and final component of emotion is motivated action. Emotions often seem to contain the impulse to act in certain ways appropriate to the particular emotion. For example, when angry, you may feel a strong urge to hit out at someone in some way, when in love to seek out the company of your loved one and get as close as you possibly can to him or her, and when afraid you may feel the strong desire to run away, literally or metaphorically.

A currently popular view is that the evolutionary functions of different emotions serve particular survival-related goal systems and put the organism in a state of readiness for dealing with situations of particular kinds (e.g., Smith & Ellsworth, 1985). According to this perspective, emotions should be seen as inherently *motivational* states, serving particular functions. For example, the evolutionary goal of anger might be to protect oneself from antagonists, so the angry state prepares the organism for aggression and retaliation. Similarly, fear has obvious survival relevance in preparing for rapid escape from a dangerous situation. The direct survival implications of emotions such as happiness, embarrassment, sadness, and so on, however, are a little harder to locate, and it may be that the behaviours associated with these emotions serve social rather than evolutionary functions. For example, we may get embarrassed to distance ourselves from a potential negative evaluation in public: the urge to hide or become invisible may reflect the socially produced need to avoid being a focus of other people's attention at such times (e.g., Modigliani, 1971).

SEQUENCES OF EMOTION: THE INTERNAL STRUCTURE OF EMOTIONAL EXPERIENCE

I have considered some of the factors that are symptomatic of emotion. I shall now look at these same variables again, but this time discussing their possible participation in the causation of emotional experience. My approach will be to consider the roles these factors have been assigned by different theorists in explaining how emotional experience is produced. Finally, I shall attempt to integrate the insights of these alternative models into a more general model of the emotional syndrome as a whole.

Factor 1: appraisal

The first and most central factor in the causation of emotion relates to the evaluation of some situation or event, based on the process of appraisal. Appraisal theorists suggest that emotions are rarely direct reactions to stimulus qualities. Rather, what gives an object emotional impact is its relevance to the individual's personal concerns. Lazarus (1984), for example, argued that before it can cause an emotion, a stimulus, event, or encounter must be interpreted and evaluated to weigh up its personal significance.

An experiment by Lazarus's research team (Speisman, Lazarus, Mordkoff, & Davison, 1964) provides an illustration of how emotional response might depend upon appraisal. The unfortunate subjects in this study were shown a movie depicting a tribal ritual called "subincision" in which adolescent males undergo an apparently painful operation on their genitals. The film was found to be emotionally unpleasant to watch, producing autonomic and self-report reactions of stress. However, these reactions could be reduced by including a soundtrack suggesting an "anthropological perspective" which encouraged subjects to interpret the depicted events in terms of the insights they provided into an alien culture. Correspondingly, a soundtrack emphasizing the trauma of the ritual increased stress reactions. The authors argued that the different soundtracks modified subjects' ongoing appraisal of the emotional content of the movie, allowing them to interpret the material as more or less threatening, and thus intensify or alleviate their emotional reaction.

In contemporary emotion theory, appraisal is the central explanatory concept. Lazarus (1991) has even argued that appraisal is both a necessary and sufficient condition for emotional experience. Other theorists suggest that other variables have a role to play in determining emotional experience (Parkinson & Manstead, 1992). I shall consider some of the other factors that might influence emotional experience, before moving on to a discussion of whether emotion is as exclusively dependent on appraisal as Lazarus has suggested.

Factor 2: arousal

According to William James (1898), who is often credited with devising the first modern psychological theory of emotion, the common-sense idea of how emotion is caused, where a situational encounter directly produces emotional feeling, actually gets things backwards (see Figure 1a and Figure 1b):

> Our natural way of thinking ... is that the mental perception of some fact excites the mental affection called the emotion, and that this latter state of mind gives rise to the bodily expression. My thesis, on the contrary, is that *the bodily changes follow directly the perception of the exciting fact, and that our feeling of the same changes as they occur IS the emotion.* Common sense says, we lose our fortune, are sorry and weep; we meet a bear, are frightened and run; we are insulted by a rival, are angry and strike. The hypothesis here to be defended says that this order of sequence is incorrect ... and that the more rational statement is that we feel sorry because we cry, angry because we strike, afraid because we tremble, and not that we cry, strike, or tremble because we are sorry, angry, fearful, as the case may be. (p. 449, emphasis in original)

James (1898) argued that the differences between emotions are a direct result of the different patterns of physiological response associated with them. According to James, seeing something frightening instinctively triggers a whole set of reactions in our bodies. The particular pattern of these reactions is felt by us consciously and experienced as the particular emotion of fear.

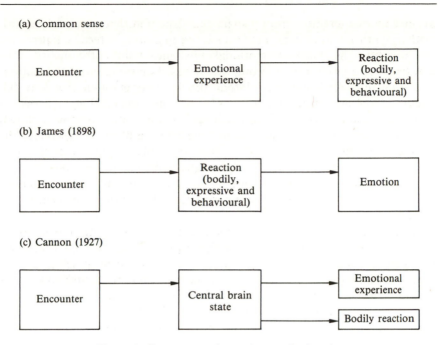

(a) Common sense

(b) James (1898)

(c) Cannon (1927)

Figure 1 Sequences of emotion: early theories

For example, our feelings of fear might be based on the feeling of raised blood pressure, tightening of our muscles, a certain sensation in our guts.

One of the main problems with James's theory, as pointed out by Cannon (1927), is that the physiological changes that accompany a wide variety of emotions are actually very similar, and certainly not distinct enough to differentiate widely contrasting subjective states such as euphoria and anger. Cannon's alternative theory represented a slight return towards the common-sense view of emotion. Cannon's idea was that emotional encounters directly triggered a central brain process in the thalamus, which had two simultaneous and independent outputs, one to the arousal system which prepared the body to cope with the emergency, and the second to the cortex where the conscious experience of the emotion was registered (see Figure 1c). Thus the symptoms of quickened pulse, sweating, and so on, were simply side-effects of energy mobilization in preparation for responding to emergency, and were irrelevant to the subjective awareness of emotion. In defence of this position, Cannon pointed out that sensory feedback from the body's periphery was simply too slow and too vaguely registered to allow it a causal role in the production of rapid and differentiated emotional experience.

Schachter (1964) revived and revised James's idea that emotions are dependent on feedback from bodily changes, but also accepted Cannon's arguments that emotions mostly share the same bodily response of generalized sympathetic arousal. Schachter believed that arousal feedback provided the subjective "heat" behind emotional experience, but that the quality of the emotion was derived from a second factor based on situational information.

Specifically, Schachter argued that the kind of emotion that was felt depended on how arousal was interpreted and explained by the person experiencing it. In this view, if you believe that your state of arousal is caused by a wild animal that is chasing you, then you are likely to experience the state as fear. However, if you think that your arousal is triggered by the close presence of somebody attractive, you might well come to feel your reaction as love, or at least as lust, for that person. In other words, emotion consists of an *attribution* of arousal to an emotionally relevant situational cause (see Figure 2).

If Schachter's theory is correct, then it is possible to change the emotions that people experience simply by modifying the way that they interpret their arousal reactions; in a famous experiment, this is exactly what Schachter and Singer (1962) tried to do. In the study, the first thing Schachter and Singer had to do was to get people into a state of arousal that was not linked to any emotional state. They achieved this by injecting the experimental subjects with adrenaline, under the pretext that it was a new vitamin compound called suproxin, whose effects the experimenters were testing (in a control condition, the suproxin injection was actually a saline placebo). Second, the investigators had to convince the subjects that their experienced arousal was produced by either emotional or non-emotional causes. They managed this by accurately informing some subjects that the injection would bring about all the usual side-effects of arousal including heart-rate increase, a rise in body temperature, and so on, but by deceiving other subjects that the injection would have no side-effects (or side-effects unrelated to an arousal reaction). These latter misinformed subjects, therefore, were supposed to

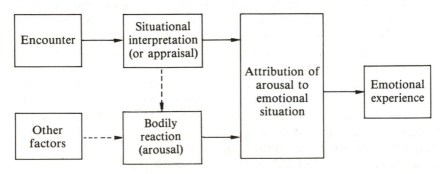

Note: Broken lines represent linkages that are possible rather than necessary

Figure 2   Schachter's two-factor theory

experience arousal symptoms without knowing their source, and according to the theory should experience emotion depending upon how they came to explain their felt symptoms.

Schachter and Singer manipulated their subjects' emotional explanations for unexplained arousal by putting them into different situations. This was done while subjects were supposedly waiting for the vitamin compound to be absorbed. Each subject waited with another supposed subject who was actually an accomplice of the experimenter and who acted in one of two different ways, contrived to convey contrasting emotional situations.

In the first condition, the accomplice tried to create a general atmosphere of *euphoria*. For example, he improvised a basket-ball game with screwed up pieces of paper and a waste-bin, made paper planes, aimed a makeshift catapult at a tower he had built from some folders, and finally discovered some conveniently concealed hula hoops and started playing with one of them, leaving the other within easy reach of the subject.

In the second condition, the situational manipulation was intended to occasion the emotion of *anger*. Here, the real subject and the accomplice were asked to fill in a questionnaire while waiting for the suproxin to be absorbed. This questionnaire started out fairly inoffensively, asking about the subject's age, sex, and so on. From then on, the questions became increasingly personal and insulting. For example, one item asked: "With how many men (other than your father) has your mother had extra-marital relationships?" The only response alternatives provided were: "4 and under"; "5 to 9"; and "10 and over"! The accomplice made irritated comments as he answered the questions. Finally, his acted annoyance reached such a pitch that he tore up the questionnaire and threw it on the floor, shouting: "I'm not wasting any more time. I'm getting my books and leaving".

The extent to which subjects got caught up in the general emotional atmosphere of these two contrasting situations was assessed by observers who watched their behaviour from behind one-way glass. Subjects also made self-ratings of their emotional state. According to the experimental predictions, the only subjects who should have got emotional as a function of the accomplice's behaviour were those who had been injected with adrenaline but not warned about the effects it would have on their bodies. Subjects given an accurate warning about symptoms would have a perfectly good non-emotional explanation of their felt reaction and therefore would not take on the mood of the accomplice. Correspondingly, subjects who had been injected with a placebo should have experienced no extra arousal and therefore no increase in emotion. If either arousal or an emotional explanation for arousal were missing, then no emotion should have resulted. On the other hand, subjects who experienced unexplained arousal should have attributed their symptoms to the emotional characteristics of the situation and taken on the emotional state of euphoria or anger depending upon which emotion the accomplice acted out.

In fact, these predicted differences in emotional experience failed to emerge as clearly as Schachter and Singer might have hoped. Although subjects correctly informed about the effects of the injection consistently reported less emotion than those given incorrect side-effects information, subjects who had been injected with an inert placebo did not always differ significantly from misinformed aroused subjects. In other words, the administration of adrenaline did not make a reliable difference to the emotional experience of subjects. An even bigger problem was that subjects in the anger condition did not generally report their mood as negative at all: even when injected with adrenaline, misinformed of side-effects, and subjected to a humiliating questionnaire, they still rated themselves as mildly happy! Subsequent attempts to replicate the study have been similarly inconclusive (see Reisenzein, 1983, for a review).

Although the evidence for Schachter's theory is not completely convincing, his theory was historically influential because it suggested a potentially important role for interpersonal variables in the constitution of emotional experience. Previously, social factors were thought to play a role only in modifying the *expression* of an unchanged underlying biologically determined state (e.g., Ekman's concept of *display rules*), but after Schachter, theorists began to recognize the possibility that social interactions and interpersonal roles could directly shape the experience of emotion (e.g., Averill, 1980).

The second main influence of two-factor theory has been on self-attributional accounts of emotion (e.g., Laird & Bresler, 1992). Schachter suggested that emotion is based on an inferential process through which people come to the conclusion that they are emotional on the basis of the evidence that is available to them. If they believe that a plausibly emotional object has caused them to become aroused, they will conclude that their feelings about that object must be quite strong. This self-perception analysis (Bem, 1972) suggests that other sources of emotionally relevant information might similarly affect emotional judgements. Such information might arise, for example, from awareness of facial expression, or feedback from emotional action.

Factor 3: facial expression

Unlike the signals available from the autonomic nervous system, which as we have seen are too diffuse to provide diagnostic information about emotional quality, facial expressive patterns show at least some consistent relations with specific emotions. Several theorists have suggested that feedback from facial expression is an important source of emotional feelings (e.g., Izard, 1971; Tomkins, 1962).

Darwin (1872) was the first to suggest that facial responses might affect as well as reflect emotional experience. He argued that "the free expression by outward signs of an emotion intensifies it. On the other hand, the repression as far as possible of all outward signs softens our emotions" (p. 22).

Many studies have supported Darwin's insight, showing that facial expressions have a small but reliable influence on the strength of emotional reactions. One of the most convincing demonstrations of a facial feedback effect was provided by Strack, Martin, and Stepper (1988). These investigators apparently succeeded in manipulating facial expression without subjects' awareness. Subjects were told that the study was an investigation of how disabled people manage to perform various tasks using parts of the body that are not normally used for these tasks. In the study, subjects were asked to write while holding the pen in their mouth. One of their assigned tasks was to rate how funny a series of cartoons was. While performing this task, some of the subjects were told to hold the pen between their teeth, a position which puts the face in an expression close to a smile, while others were told they could use only their lips to hold the pen, effectively preventing them from smiling and encouraging more of a frowning face. It was found that subjects who held the pen between their teeth rated their amusement at the cartoons as significantly higher than those who held the pen using their lips. Thus, it seems that our emotional reactions to emotional material can be influenced partially by the expression we have on our face.

How does facial expression affect emotional experience? In Laird's (1974) original facial feedback experiment, one subject explained his reaction as follows: "When my jaw was clenched and my brows down I tried not to be angry but it just fit the position. . . . I found my thoughts wandering to things that made me angry which is sort of silly I guess. I knew I was in an experiment and knew I had no reason to feel that way, but I just lost control" (p. 480). Clearly, this subject was perfectly aware that the position of his face resembled a frown, and this recognition consciously triggered thoughts relating to anger, which in turn made him feel a little more angry. Lard interpreted his results in terms of self-perception theory, arguing that people's emotional feelings are based partly on the evidence from their own facial expressions.

This kind of inferential process seems less likely in Strack, Martin, and Stepper's study where subjects were apparently unaware that they were smiling or frowning. It may be that facial expressions influence emotional experience to the extent that they contribute to, or interfere with, the natural way of reacting in an emotional situation. However, the influence is not usually very great and has been demonstrated only with respect to a limited range of emotions such as amusement and pain.

Factor 4: action readiness

According to Frijda (1986), the awareness of desires and impulses to action is a vital part of the experience of emotion. In this view, active emotions such as anger and fear are characterized by the feeling of action readiness, whereas the experience of more passive emotions such as sorrow and despair includes feelings of loss of interest and disinclination for action. In support of this position, strong correlations have been obtained between self-ascriptions of emotions, and self-reports of modes of action readiness (e.g., Frijda, Kuipers, & ter Schure, 1989). Reports also suggest that the experience of action readiness in emotion is felt as involuntary and impulsive rather than deliberate and controlled. The urge to act in a certain way or to refrain from action seems to be something that comes over people, rather than something they choose to do. Frijda calls this the felt *control precedence* of an emotion and believes that it can be seen as a further defining feature of what is taken to be emotional experience.

Synthesis: four-factor theory

I have considered several possible causal routes to the production of an emotional experience, with different theorists assigning priority to different categories of variable from the four factors of emotion. The reader may feel entitled at this point to ask which of these sequences is the correct one. The simple answer to this is the appraisal sequence: emotion is determined mainly by our evaluations and interpretations of the personal significance of events. However, a more complete answer based on the current state of our knowledge is that most of the suggested sequences may be applicable under certain circumstances. Feedback from any of the four factors of the patterned emotional response may occasionally contribute to the strength or quality of the experience.

To summarize my conclusions from the present section, there are two main kinds of theories of how emotion is caused. The first set of theories focus on how the situation leads to emotion, and are typically based on the concept of cognitive appraisal. The second set concentrate on the role of bodily reactions in emotional experience and rely on notions of feedback. Of course, appraisal and feedback theories are not necessarily mutually exclusive. For example, bodily reactions are often caused by appraisal of the situation (Smith, 1989), and the effects these reactions have on emotion in turn often reflect the way they influence the appraisal process. If you notice your heart is pounding, you may look for a plausible emotional cause for this reaction in the situation, which you will then reappraise in more emotional terms. Laird and Bresler (1992) suggest that feedback or self-perception theory explains how the subjective experience of emotion is constructed out of the various sources of emotional information, but appraisal theory accounts for the bodily changes that produce this feedback information. However, factors other than appraisal may also sometimes influence the various sources of feedback and make their independent contribution to the causation of emotion (see Figure 3).

16

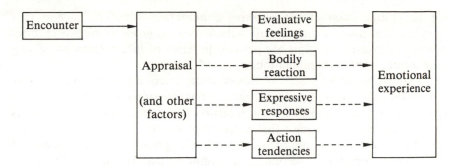

Note: Broken lines represent linkages that are possible rather than necessary

Figure 3 A four-factor theory of emotion

Another way of viewing the emotional process is to see all four kinds of phenomena as manifestations of a common underlying process (Frijda, 1986). From this perspective, the process of emotion can be specified as the impact of a stimulus event, consisting of an appraisal of that event leading to an effect upon action readiness. Feeling is primarily the conscious result of that appraisal. Emotional expression, motivated behaviour, and physiological change are all manifestations of the state of action-readiness, and awareness of these factors also contributes to feeling. In this view, the feeling of anger, for example, is a specific patterned motivational state containing an appraisal of other-blame which directly implies a readiness to hit out at this other person, and is expressed through the body and on the face. In other words, rather than seeing emotional experience as constructed out of various channels of feedback information, we can see emotion as an integrated evaluative process which already includes the various aspects of the response syndrome.

EMOTION AND COGNITION

In this chapter so far, I have tried to understand emotion by looking at it from the inside by asking what kinds of things emotions are, what constituent components they have, and how these components might fit together to make an emotional experience. Finally, I shall consider emotion's external relations with another important psychological function, that of cognition. Thus, I shall try to get a final fix on what emotion is by mapping its relative position in general psychological theory.

In common sense, emotion is often considered as the opposite of rational, considered thought. When emotional, we act impulsively in the heat of the moment rather than coolly calculating the best course of action, the heart rather than the head becomes the crucial metaphoric organ controlling what we do (Lutz, 1988). These intuitive connotations seem to suggest that emotional phenomena might fall outside the range of cognitive theories whose explanatory concepts are phrased in terms of information processing and formal symbol manipulation.

However, as we have seen in this chapter, many psychologists currently believe that the way we feel emotionally about something is crucially dependent upon the way we evaluate and interpret that thing cognitively. Lazarus (1991), for example, argues that emotion is always preceded by cognitive appraisal which determines the quality and the quantity of the response. In other words, emotion is secondary to cognitive activity. Against this view, Zajonc (1980) has suggested that affective reactions can arise in the absence of any prior cognitive processing, and more generally, that cognition and emotion are fundamentally separate systems just as common sense appears to suggest.

One of Zajonc's examples can be used to illustrate his point. He argues that when we meet people, we are sometimes aware of whether or not we like them even before we have remembered who they are. Similarly, Zajonc suggests that our affective judgements of the pleasantness or unpleasantness of all kinds of objects can be immediate and independent of any cognitive interpretation.

There are two obvious problems with this account. First, although most people would accept that emotional reactions sometimes arise without any prior *conscious* evaluative or interpretational work, this does not mean that no information processing of any kind has occurred. In fact, it would be difficult to explain our different emotional reactions to different situations if no recognition processes came first. Zajonc would argue that this recognition may sometimes be affective rather than cognitive. Lazarus (1984), on the other hand, would say that any recognition of the personal significance of an encounter is *appraisal* by definition, even though this appraisal may often be unconscious and automatic. Stating the controversy this way suggests that the only real disagreement between Lazarus and Zajonc may relate to how the processes preceding emotional reaction are defined. In fact, appraisal need not be seen in *purely* cognitive terms anyway (e.g., Parrott & Sabini, 1989), since it clearly includes a strong evaluative element.

The second problem with Zajonc's analysis is that it is not clear whether he is really talking about *emotion* or simply about *affect*. Lazarus (1984) argued as follows: "Cognitive activity is a necessary precondition of emotion because to experience an emotion, people must comprehend – whether in the form of a primitive evaluative perception or a highly differentiated symbolic process – that their well-being is implicated in a transaction, for better or worse" (p. 124). If Lazarus's analysis of what emotion involves is correct, then much of Zajonc's argument does not concern emotional phenomena at all. Like Lazarus, I have argued above that it is hard to imagine a genuine emotional state that does not include at its centre an evaluative relation to some intentional object. However, in my opinion, the issue of causality is not quite as simple as Lazarus sometimes seems to imply. It may be that other non-cognitive factors, such as bodily and facial feedback, also contribute to the causation of both appraisal and emotion (Parkinson & Manstead, 1992).

CONCLUSION

Like the psychology of emotion itself, this chapter began with an apparently simple question: "What is an emotion?" (cf. James, 1884). Much of what I have written here helps to answer this question. An emotion is a relatively short-term, evaluative state focused on a particular intentional object (a person, an event, or a state of affairs). Good examples are anger, fear, love, and hate. Emotional reactions typically include many of the following four components: appraisal of the situation, bodily response, facial expression, and changes in action readiness. None of these factors is completely necessary for emotional experience, but it would be implausible to describe as emotional any state that included none of them. Emotion can be seen as the unfolding pattern of interrelationships of these aspects, as the subjective experience of the episode, or as an underlying process that determines the whole syndrome. In any case, the investigation of emotion requires a range of perspectives (e.g., cognitive, physiological, ethological, and social), all of which have a role to play in our overall understanding of the phenomenon (Averill, 1992). In this chapter, I have tried to give a flavour of the spectrum of possible relevant analyses.

ACKNOWLEDGEMENT

This chapter has been influenced in many not always obvious ways by the work of Nico Frijda, whose contribution is gratefully and respectfully acknowledged.

FURTHER READING

Averill, J. R. (1982). *Anger and aggression: An essay on emotion.* New York: Springer.

Clark, M. (Ed.) (1992) *Review of personality and social psychology: vol. 13. Emotion.* Beverly-Hills, CA: Sage.

Frijda, N. H. (1986). *The emotions.* Cambridge: Cambridge University Press.

Lazarus, R. S. (1991). *Emotion and adaptation.* Oxford: Oxford University Press.

Ortony, A., Clore, G. L., & Collins, A. (1988). *The cognitive structure of emotions.* Cambridge: Cambridge University Press.

REFERENCES

Arnold, M. B. (1960). *Emotion and personality: vol. 1. Psychological aspects*. New York: Columbia University Press.

Averill, J. R. (1974). An analysis of psychophysiological symbolism and its influence on theories of emotion. *Journal for the Theory of Social Behaviour, 4*, 147–190.

Averill, J. R. (1980). A constructivist view of emotions. In R. Plutchik & H. Kellerman (Eds) *Emotions: Theory, research, and experience* (vol. 1, pp. 305–339). New York: Academic Press.

Averill, J. R. (1992). The structural bases of emotional behavior: A metatheoretical analysis. In M. S. Clark (Ed.) *Review of personality and social psychology: Emotion* (vol. 13, pp. 1–24). Newbury Park, CA: Sage.

Bem, D. J. (1972). Self-perception theory. In L. Festinger (Ed.) *Advances in experimental social psychology* (vol. 6, pp. 1–62). New York: Academic Press.

Cannon, W. B. (1927). The James-Lange theory of emotions: A critical examination and an alternative theory. *American Journal of Psychology, 39*, 106–124.

Cannon, W. B. (1929). *Bodily changes in pain, hunger, fear, and rage* (2nd edn). New York: Appleton.

Clark, M. S., & Isen, A. M. (1982). Toward understanding the relationship between feeling states and social behavior. In A. H. Hastorf & A. M. Isen (Eds) *Cognitive social psychology* (pp. 73–108). New York: Elsevier.

Clore, G. L., & Ortony, A. (1991). What more is there to emotion concepts than prototypes? *Journal of Personality and Social Psychology, 60*, 48–50.

Darwin, C. R. (1872). *The expression of emotions in man and animals*. London: John Murray.

Ekman, P., & Friesen, W. V. (1971). Constants across cultures in the face and emotion. *Journal of Personality and Social Psychology, 17*, 124–129.

Ekman, P., Levenson, R. W., & Friesen, W. V. (1983). Autonomic nervous system activity distinguishes among emotions. *Science, 221*, 1208–1210.

Fehr, B., & Russell, J. A. (1984). Concept of emotion viewed from a prototype perspective. *Journal of Experimental Psychology: General, 113*, 464–486.

Frijda, N. H. (1986). *The emotions*. Cambridge: Cambridge University Press.

Frijda, N. H., Kuipers, P., & ter Schure, E. (1989). Relations among emotion, appraisal, and emotional action readiness. *Journal of Personality and Social Psychology, 57*, 212–228.

Harré, R. (Ed.) (1986). *The social construction of emotions*. New York: Basil Blackwell.

Izard, C. E. (1971). *The face of emotion*. New York: Appleton-Century-Crofts.

James, W. (1884). What is an emotion? *Mind, 9*, 188–205.

James, W. (1898). *The principles of psychology* (vol. 2). London: Macmillan.

Laird, J. D. (1974). Self-attribution of emotion: The effects of facial expression on the quality of emotional experience. *Journal of Personality and Social Psychology, 29*, 475–486.

Laird, J. D., & Bresler, C. (1992). The process of emotional experience: A self-perception theory. In M. S. Clark (Ed.) *Review of personality and social psychology: Emotion* (vol. 13, pp. 213–234). Newbury Park, CA: Sage.

Lazarus, R. S. (1968). Emotions and adaptation. In W. J. Arnold (Ed.) *Nebraska symposium on motivation* (vol. 16. pp. 175–265). Lincoln, NE: University of Nebraska Press.

Lazarus, R. S. (1984). On the primacy of cognition. *American Psychologist, 39*, 124–129.

Lazarus, R. S. (1991). *Emotion and adaptation*. Oxford: Oxford University Press.

Lutz, C. (1988). *Unnatural emotions*. Chicago, IL: University of Chicago Press.

Modigliani, A. (1971). Embarrassment, facework, and eye-contact: Testing a theory of embarrassment. *Journal of Personality and Social Psychology*, *17*, 15–24.

Nieuwenhuyse, B., Offenberg, L., & Frijda, N. H. (1987). Subjective emotion and reported body experience. *Motivation and Emotion*, *11*, 169–182.

Ortony, A., & Turner, T. J. (1991). What's basic about basic emotions? *Psychological Review*, *97*, 315–331.

Parkinson, B., & Manstead, A. S. R. (1992). Appraisal as a cause of emotion. In M. S. Clark (Ed.) *Review of personality and social psychology* (vol. 13, pp. 122–149). New York: Sage.

Parrott, W. G., & Sabini, J. (1989). On the "emotional" qualities of certain types of cognition: A reply to arguments for the independence of cognition and affect. *Cognitive Therapy and Research*, *13*, 49–65.

Reisenzein, R. (1983). The Schachter theory of emotion: Two decades later. *Psychological Bulletin*, *94*, 239–264.

Rimé, B., Philippot, P., & Cisamolo, D. (1990). Social schemata of peripheral changes in emotion. *Journal of Personality and Social Psychology*, *59*, 38–49.

Rosch, E. (1978). Principles of categorization. In E. Rosch & B. B. Lloyd (Eds) *Cognition and categorization* (pp. 27–48). Hillsdale, NJ: Lawrence Erlbaum.

Schachter, S. (1964). The interaction of cognitive and physiological determinants of emotional state. In L. Festinger (Ed.) *Advances in experimental social psychology* (vol. 1, pp. 49–80). New York: Academic Press.

Schachter, S., & Singer, J. E. (1962). Cognitive, social, and physiological determinants of emotional state. *Psychological Review*, *69*, 379–399.

Scherer, K. R. (1986). Vocal affect expression: A review and a model for future research. *Psychological Bulletin*, *99*, 143–165.

Smith, C. A. (1989). Dimensions of appraisal and physiological response in emotion. *Journal of Personality and Social Psychology*, *56*, 339–353.

Smith, C. A., & Ellsworth, P. C. (1985). Patterns of cognitive appraisal in emotion. *Journal of Personality and Social Psychology*, *48*, 813–838.

Smith, C. A., & Lazarus, R. S. (1990). Emotion and adaptation. In L. A. Pervin (Ed.) *Handbook of personality: Theory and research* (pp. 609–637). New York: Guilford.

Speisman, J. C., Lazarus, R. S., Mordkoff, A., & Davison, L. (1964). Experimental reduction of stress based on ego-defense theory. *Journal of Abnormal and Social Psychology*, *68*, 367–380.

Strack, F., Martin, L. L., & Stepper, S. (1988). Inhibiting and facilitating conditions of the human smile: A non-obtrusive test of facial feedback hypothesis. *Journal of Personality and Social Psychology*, *54*, 768–777.

Tomkins, S. S. (1962). *Affect, imagery, consciousness: vol. 1 The positive affects*. New York: Springer.

Zajonc, R. B. (1980). Feeling and thinking: Preferences need no inferences. *American Psychologist*, *35*, 151–175.

2

HUNGER AND APPETITE

John E. Blundell and Andrew J. Hill
University of Leeds, England

Hunger and appetite are phenomena that have always been central to the study of motivation. They both belong to the domain of psychological inquiry that seeks to find the reasons underlying the actions of human beings and animals. The terms "hunger" and "appetite" are widely used both in scientific literature and in non-technical discourse to refer to states and processes that guide food consumption. That is, they describe the drive or the motivational force that constrains us to eat particular foods within a certain pattern of eating. However, we should not think of hunger and appetite as simple entities with a simple causal relationship to eating behaviour. Hunger and appetite are themselves quite different and complex phenomena. By examining their structure and the way in which they operate we shall be drawn into an examination of the mechanisms that control eating and which, in turn, exert an influence over body weight. Accordingly, this exploration of the control of the motivation to eat will lead into a consideration of disorders of motivation (over- and under-eating) and, in addition, disorders of body weight. Indeed, a part of the impetus to study hunger and appetite as motivational forces comes from the need to understand and treat motivation when it is poorly regulated.

In order to generate a clear understanding of hunger and appetite, one major task is to define their relationships with environmental happenings, physiological states, and objectively measured food consumption. Initially, it is necessary to define the terms. Although the reader may discover some disagreement among scientists about the precise meanings of the terms, the following descriptions provide working definitions.

Appetite can refer to the sum total of processes influencing the expression of the willingness to eat. Appetite is the global phenomenon influenced by cultural, economic, physiological, and cognitive factors. Hence it is appropriate to speak about the regulation of appetite and to consider the factors that influence this regulation. It is not necessary to use appetite in any more precise technical sense.

The logical status of the term *hunger* needs clarification, for it is clear that the term is used in more than one sense by psychologists. On the one hand, hunger is a motivational construct with the logical status of a mediating concept or intervening variable (Royce, 1963). That is, the term refers to an explanatory principle which is inferred from other directly observable and measurable events. In this sense the term helps in understanding the motivational processes. On the other hand, hunger may be used to refer to certain conscious sensations or feelings linked to a desire to obtain and eat food. This is the sense in which lay people understand the notion of hunger. It is necessary to emphasize the distinction between the psychological process of hunger with relevance for motivational theory, on the one hand, and the conscious sensation of hunger on the other. It is these hunger sensations that probably exert motivational pressure on behaviour, and it is these that researchers attempt to capture by means of rating scales and other devices.

Throughout this chapter, the term hunger will be used to represent a subjective experience or feeling that is associated with the desire to eat and obtain food. From a functional point of view, hunger achieves a purpose as that nagging, irritating feeling whose presence constantly serves to stimulate thoughts about food and eating. Hunger can also be present as a latent disposition which becomes activated in the presence of food stimuli. Hunger is therefore useful and reminds us that the body needs food. In this way hunger can be seen to possess a clear biological function.

How important is hunger in the expression of appetite? To what extent is appetite influenced by physiological and environmental factors? What role do cognition and attitudes play in changing the intensity or direction of appetite? How does nutrition influence the strength of the disposition to eat which is the essence of appetite? The answers to these questions will provide a framework for understanding appetite as a motivational phenomenon.

PHYSIOLOGICAL AND ENVIRONMENTAL INTERACTIONS

Appetite represents the constellation of forces that control eating, and eating is an activity that links alterations in the physiological domain (under the skin) with events taking place in a domain beyond the skin (the environment). Indeed, eating behaviour represents a particularly intimate form of interaction between organisms and their environments, for it involves consumption of part of the environment, which in turn forms part of the organism and influences the interaction. Moreover, eating is an episodic activity and the processes of appetite control must account for this.

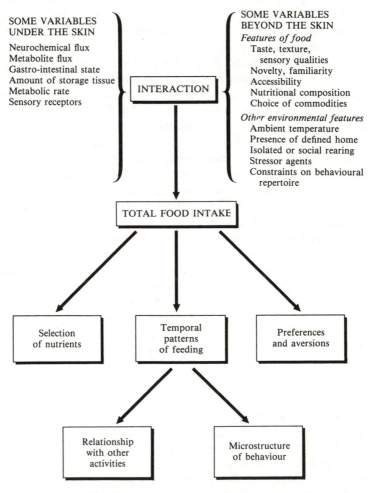

Figure 1 The expression of appetite (food intake, temporal patterns, nutrient selection, etc.) reflecting an interaction between internal and external factors

24

The particular patterns of eating observed at any time represent an interaction between two constellations of factors (Blundell, 1979). Figure 1 draws attention to the fact that eating depends not only on the neurochemical and metabolic state of organisms but also on environmental features such as the taste, texture, novelty, accessibility, and choice of food, and on other external features such as the presence of other organisms. This notion of appetite as the consequence of an interaction provides a framework for thinking about appetite in animals as well as in humans. Indeed, Figure 1 emphasizes the way in which food consumption can be broken down into specific components (nutrient selection, micro-structure of behaviour, etc.) so as to diagnose the effects of various factors on the expression of appetite. The pattern of eating provides a sensitive way of assessing the impact of physiological or environmental features (Blundell, 1984). Of course, for humans, the subjective experiences or cognitions surrounding eating can similarly be regarded as being constructed out of physiological signals and the characteristics of the external environment (Blundell, 1981). Reynolds (1976) has referred to these cognitions as culturally defined knowledge entering the mind to give contours to the world, thus making sense out of physiological functioning.

As a first stage in understanding appetite, the interactional concept is important, for it lets us know that the phenomenon is not controlled by a single dominant cause. The analysis of appetite will therefore require an appreciation on the interrelationships among a number of factors from quite separate domains. This approach is equally important for the study of appetite in animals and in humans. However, for the investigation of human appetite a further conceptual scheme is appropriate.

APPETITE AND BODY WEIGHT REGULATION

It has been noted above that appetite can be considered a phenomenon that links biological happenings (under the skin) with environmental happenings (beyond the skin). This interaction has implications for the regulation of body weight. This is inevitable because energy balance is dependent upon the relationship between energy intake (food consumption) and energy expenditure (physical activity, energy used to maintain bodily processes, and energy involved in the processing and storage of consumed food). A positive energy balance (intake greater than expenditure) means that body weight will be gained, whereas a negative energy balance leads to weight loss. Any factors that influence appetite will naturally adjust energy intake, and this will alter energy balance. It is normally considered that body weight is a variable subject to homeostatic control. That is, body weight is biologically regulated. However, because appetite is also influenced by environmental factors, an examination of the principles of weight regulation should tell us something about the strength of biological and environmental influences on appetite. What basic principles can be uncovered?

Figure 2 illustrates how appetite is shaped by the principles of biological regulation and environmental adaptation. All living organisms require food (a nutrition supply) for growth and maintenance of tissues. This supply is achieved through eating. The expression of this behaviour is controlled according to the state of the biological system. A complex system of signals operates to ensure the appropriate direction and quality of this (eating) behaviour. The extension of Claude Bernard's principle of homeostasis to include behaviour is often referred to as the behavioural regulation of internal states (Richter, 1943). However, the expression of behaviour is also subject to environmental demands, and behaviour is therefore adapted in the face of particular circumstances.

In the case of human appetite, attention must be given to the conscious and deliberate (external) control over behaviour. Human beings can decide to alter their own behaviour in order to meet particular objectives, for example, a display of moral conviction (political hunger strike) or a demonstration of aesthetic achievement (dieting). In both of these examples, eating is curtailed with an ensuing interruption of the nutritional supply. Regulatory mechanisms will tend to oppose this undersupply and generate a drive to eat. In the technically advanced cultures of Europe and North America, the nutritional supply may be adjusted in another way. The existence of an abundant supply of palatable, energy-dense food promotes overconsumption. This in turn, in an interaction with genetic susceptibility, leads to an increase in fat deposition (Bouchard, 1985). However, an oversupply of calories leading to the deposition of body fat does not generate a biological drive to undereat. Hence, the operation of the regulatory system is not symmetrical:

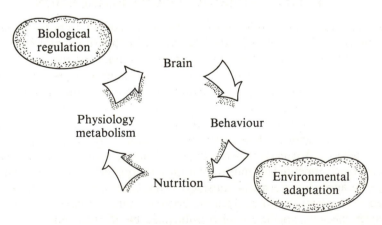

Figure 2   Schema indicating the way in which eating contributes to biological regulation and environmental adaptation

there is a strong defence against undernutrition and only weak response to the effects of overnutrition.

These principles appear to tell us that appetite is actively stimulated whenever there is any reduction in food intake and a threat to bodily integrity. However, the appetite control system can passively accept an excess of food (or at least of some types of foods) which in turn can lead to a positive energy balance. The existence of these principles may help to explain the increasing prevalence of obesity in many affluent cultures in the final decade of the twentieth century.

Because the control of appetite is so fundamental to the existence of all living organisms, we can expect that the principles governing this control will have obvious functional value. Do the principles make sense? For human beings it can be supposed that during most of the tens of thousands of years of human evolution the biggest problem facing humankind was the scarcity of food (Boyd Eaton & Konner, 1985). Hence, powerful mechanisms will have developed to signal this deficit and to generate an appropriate motivational response. However, the existence of an abundance of food, highly palatable and readily available, is a very recent development in evolutionary terms. Accordingly, it is unlikely that evolutionary pressure has ever led to the development of mechanisms to prevent overconsumption. Indeed, the presence in the body of depots of adipose tissue (fat) ensures that any excessive intake of calories can be readily accommodated. Consequently, we should not necessarily expect to find a simple symmetrical relationship between appetite control and body weight regulation. This asymmetry may help us to understand the way in which appetite is deregulated in the eating and weight disorders.

APPETITE AS THE OUTPUT OF A BIOPSYCHOLOGICAL SYSTEM

One useful strategy for understanding the variety of factors that influence the expression of appetite is to consider the operation of a biopsychological system. This system incorporates the interactions between physiology and the environment set out in Figure 1, and includes the principles of regulation described in Figure 2. A simple outline of the biopsychological system for appetite control is sketched out in Figure 3. This conceptualization draws attention to the interrelationships between particular spheres of interest including the external environment (cultural and physical), the behavioural act of eating (quantitative and qualitative aspects), processes of ingestion and assimilation of foods, the storage and utilization of energy, brain mechanisms implicated in the control system, and mediating subjective states such as attributions and cognitions (Blundell & Hill, 1986).

The essence of the biopsychological system is that it functions in an integrated fashion. That is, an adjustment to any particular component (say, energy intake) will lead to consequences elsewhere (for example, in energy

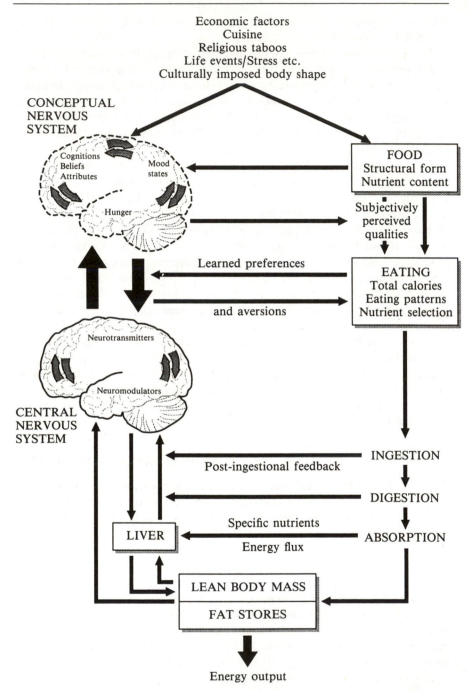

Figure 3 Conceptualization of certain major components involved in the biopsychological system underlying the expression of appetite

output). This is why dieting behaviour (self-enforced restriction of food intake) is likely to be self-defeating, because the suppression of energy consumed results in a fall in the rate at which the body utilizes energy. Energy balance tends to be preserved. The fact that eating behaviour is one component built into a biopsychological system containing many self-regulating mechanisms indicates how difficult it is to adjust eating through volitional action or by behaviour modification procedures. Although some adjustment can be made, the forces within the system exert a pressure to keep behaviour in harmony with biological actions. The force can be called motivation. One aspect of this motivation which is expressed through subjective feelings is hunger.

THE IDENTIFICATION OF HUNGER

How do we describe the experience of hunger as it occurs in everyday life? The first serious attempt to investigate this issue was made by giving people a questionnaire to complete which asked about physical sensations in a number of bodily areas, moods, urges to eat and preoccupation with thoughts of food (Monello & Mayer, 1967). The questionnaire was completed before and after eating. It was found that the observation, "I feel hungry", is typically based on the perception of bodily feelings which at times may be very strong. Gastric sensations, a hollow feeling or stomach rumbling, are frequent indicators of hunger, although people also report sensations in the mouth, throat, and head. These accompany more diffuse feelings of restlessness and excitability as well as an urge to eat. In one celebrated project known as the Minnesota experiment, a group of volunteers were placed on a semi-starvation diet for six months (Keys, Brozek, Henschel, Mickelsen, & Taylor, 1950). Their experience of hunger was extreme. Nearly two-thirds reported feeling hungry all the time and a similar proportion experienced physical discomfort due to hunger. Subjects experienced a marked increase in what was referred to as "hunger pain". For some, this pain, vaguely localized in the abdomen, was of mild discomfort. For others, it was intensely painful.

Eating changes both the pattern of physical sensations and the accompanying emotional feelings, with unpleasant and aversive sensations being replaced by more pleasant ones. So for example, an aching stomach becomes relaxed and the feeling of excitement and irritability replaced by one of contentment.

Despite a great deal of individual variability in the perception of these sensations, hunger can be associated with clear symptoms. And it is partly through reference to these that people can make judgements about the intensity of their hunger experience. The measurement of hunger, desire to eat, or urge to eat, is most commonly conducted using fixed-point or visual analogue scales. Respectively, these require the subject to choose a number from a scale or point on a line that corresponds to their current state of hunger. Careful presentation of these scales to people who understand what is being asked of them yields meaningful information. Most importantly, quantifying the subjective experience of hunger makes it a state that is amenable to scientific investigation. Consequently, hunger can be described qualitatively in terms of the sensations with which it is associated and can also be measured quantitatively. This means that the significance of hunger can be understood through its structure and by its intensity.

If hunger is the feeling that reminds us to seek food, then the consumption of food is the action that diminishes hunger and keeps it suppressed for a certain period of time, perhaps until the next meal or snack. The capacity of food to reduce the experience of hunger is called satiating power or satiating efficiency (Kissileff, 1984). This power is achieved by certain properties of the food itself engaging with various physiological and biochemical mechanisms within the body that are concerned with the processing of food once it has been ingested. The satiating power of food therefore results from a variety of biological processes and is an important factor in the control of hunger. Some foods have a greater capacity to maintain suppression over hunger than other foods.

How is hunger related to the overall control of human appetite and food consumption? The feeling of hunger is an important component in determining what we eat, how much we eat, and when we eat. However, hunger must also be seen within the context of social and physiological variables. Eating patterns are maintained by enduring habits, attitudes, and opinions about the value and suitability of foods and an overall liking for them. These factors, derived from the cultural ethos, largely determine the range of foods that will be consumed and sometimes the timing of consumption. The intensity of hunger experienced may also be determined, in part, by the culturally approved appropriateness of this feeling. However, normal hunger is more importantly associated with the events surrounding meals (so-called periprandial circumstances) and the periods between meals. Therefore, hunger can be considered to arise from an interaction between the physiological requirement of the body for food (or particular nutrients) and the capacity of food to satisfy these requirements. It follows that hunger will be successively stimulated and suppressed, giving rise to a diurnal rhythm. This rhythm, and the relationship between hunger and eating, may be altered by certain other social factors (e.g., distressing psychological events) or interrupted by some disease states.

HUNGER AND THE SATIETY CASCADE

When food consumption reduces hunger and inhibits further eating, two processes are involved. For technical precision and conceptual clarity it is useful to describe the distinction between "satiation" and "satiety". Both terms may be assigned workable operational definitions (i.e., definitions that depend on measurable events). Satiation can be regarded as the process that develops during the course of eating and that eventually brings a period of eating to an end. Accordingly, satiation can be defined in terms of the measured size of the eating episode (volume or weight of food, or energy value). Hunger declines as satiation develops and usually reaches its lowest point at the end of a meal. Satiety is defined as the state of inhibition of further eating which follows at the end of an eating episode and which arises from the consequences of food ingestion. The intensity of satiety can be measured by the duration of time elapsing until eating is recommenced, or by the amount consumed at the next meal. The strength of satiety is also measured by the duration of the suppression of hunger. As satiety weakens so hunger is restored.

In the view of some researchers, satiation and satiety can be referred to as within-meal satiety and between-meal satiety respectively (Van Itallie & Vanderweele, 1981). What mechanisms are responsible for these processes? It is clear that the mechanisms involved in reducing hunger and in continuing this suppression range from those that occur when food is initially sensed, to the effects of metabolites on bodily tissues following the digestion and absorption of food (across the wall of the intestine and into the blood stream). By definition, satiety is not an instantaneous event but occurs over a considerable time period. It is therefore useful to distinguish different phases of satiety that can be associated with different mechanisms. This concept is illustrated in Figure 4. Four mediating processes are identified: sensory,

MEDIATING PROCESSES

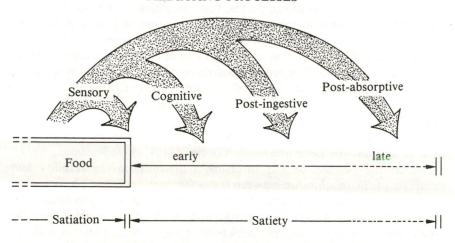

Figure 4 The satiety cascade. This diagram represents the mediating processes, arising from food consumption, which influence the feeling of hunger and the expression of appetite. One important aspect of this conceptualization is the distinction between satiation and satiety

cognitive, post-ingestive, and post-absorptive. These maintain inhibition over hunger (and eating) during the early and late phases of satiety. Sensory effects are generated through the smell, taste, temperature, and texture of food, and it is likely that these factors inhibit eating in the very short term (e.g., Rolls, Rowe, & Rolls, 1982). Cognitive effects represent the beliefs held about the properties of foods and these factors may help inhibit hunger in the short term. The category identified as post-ingestive processes includes a number of possible actions including gastric distension and rate of gastric emptying, the release of hormones such as cholecystokinin, and the stimulation of certain receptors along the gastro-intestinal tract (Mei, 1985). The post-absorptive phase of satiety includes those mechanisms arising from the action of metabolites after absorption across the intestine and into the blood stream. This category includes the action of chemicals such as glucose and amino acids, which may act directly on the brain after crossing the blood–brain barrier or which may influence the brain indirectly via neural inputs following stimulation of peripheral chemoreceptors. The most important suppression and subsequent control of hunger is brought about by post-ingestive and post-absorptive mediating processes.

CONDITIONED HUNGER

It should be kept in mind that the biopsychological system for appetite control has the capacity to learn. That is, it has the capacity to form associations between the sensory and post-absorptive characteristics of foods (e.g., Booth, 1977). This means that it will be useful to distinguish between the unconditioned effects of foods, that is, those in which the natural biological consequences of food processing are reflected upon satiety, and the conditioned effects that come into play due to the links between sensory aspects of food (particularly those that are tasted) and later metabolic effects generated by the same food. The sensory characteristics (or cues) therefore come to predict the impact that the food will later exert. Consequently, these cues can suppress hunger according to their relationship with subsequent physiological events.

This mechanism has much in common with the cue-consequence learning used to account for taste aversions (Garcia, Hankins, & Rusiniak, 1974). However, the potency of this mechanism depends on the stability and reliability of the relationship between tastes (sensory cues) and physiological effects (metabolic consequences) of food. When there is distortion or random variation between sensory characteristics and nutritional properties, then the conditioned control of hunger is weakened or lost. Learned hunger is therefore not an important factor when the food supply contains many foods with identical tastes but differing metabolic properties.

32

IS EATING CAUSED BY HUNGER?

An answer to this question can begin by considering whether hunger is a necessary or a sufficient condition for eating to occur. Because people may deliberately prevent themselves from eating in spite of hunger (fasting for moral or political conviction), hunger is not a sufficient condition. Occasions can also be imagined where a person would eat if food were particularly tempting, but where no hunger was being experienced. Therefore, it appears that hunger is neither a sufficient nor a necessary condition for eating. That is, the relationship between hunger and eating is not based on biological inevitability. However, under many circumstances there is a close relationship between the pattern of food intake and the rhythmic oscillation of hunger. Indeed, the results of many experimental studies confirm the strong relationship between the intensity of experienced hunger sensations and the amount of food consumed (e.g., De Castro & Elmore, 1988). For example, when hunger and eating have been monitored continually it has been reported that hunger ratings at the start of each hour were correlated with reported intake in the hour following each hunger rating (Mattes, 1989). The strong correlations found in almost all studies indicate that in many circumstances the measured intensity of hunger reliably predicts the amount of food that will be consumed. This fact has led to the proposal that there is a causal connection between hunger and the size of a following meal.

These observations are sufficiently strong and reliable to allow us to act as if hunger were a cause of eating. In actuality, it is probably the case that common physiological mechanisms induce changes both in hunger and in the eating response. Therefore, we can consider an appetite control system in which hunger, eating, and physiological mechanisms (of the satiety cascade) are coupled together. However, the coupling is not perfect, and there will be circumstances where, for example, a physiological treatment will change eating but not hunger. In other words, uncoupling can occur. This may take place under certain conditions of fasting or in disordered eating, and instances such as this can provide useful information about the role of hunger in the overall control of appetite.

NUTRITION, APPETITE, AND THE SATIETY CASCADE

The concept of the satiety cascade (Figure 4) implies that foods of varying nutritional composition will have different effects on the mediating processes and will therefore exert differing effects on satiation and satiety. There is considerable interest, for example, in whether the macronutrients (protein, fat, and carbohydrate) differ in their satiating efficiency or capacity to reduce hunger.

A procedure widely used to assess the action of food on satiety is the preload strategy. Precisely prepared foods (identical in taste and appearance but varying in energy and/or nutrient composition) can be consumed in the preload. Effects of consumption are then measured over varying periods by ratings of hunger and other sensations, food check-lists, accurately monitored test meals and, if necessary, food diaries. The procedure sounds simple, but the conduct of such experiments needs to be governed by a strong methodology to prevent incidental features from interfering with the monitoring process. For example, it is important to prevent the occurrence of any appetite-modulating stimuli during the interval between preload and test meal. Such interruption would obviously contaminate the measurement of the satiating efficiency of the preload.

Using the preload strategy and related procedures, it is possible to assess the satiating power of a wide variety of foods varying in nutrient composition (Blundell, Rogers, & Hill, 1988). One issue of clinical and theoretical interest is the comparative effect of carbohydrate and fat on appetite. It is clear that following consumption of carbohydrates, the digested carbohydrate influences a number of mechanisms involved in satiety. These include peripheral detectors and central nervous system monitoring of glucose. These mechanisms collectively form the basis of the energostatic control of feeding (Booth, 1972), or what has been called the caloric control of satiety (Blundell & Rogers, 1991). Although sweet carbohydrates induce some positive feedback for eating through stimulating sweet taste receptors in the mouth, this should be countered by the potent inhibitory action of the post-ingestive and post-absorptive mechanisms. Appropriate experiments should demonstrate whether or not this is the case.

One clear finding from these studies is that carbohydrates are efficient appetite suppressants. That is, they contribute markedly to the satiating efficiency of food and exert a potent effect on satiety (e.g., Rogers, Carlyle, Hill, & Blundell, 1988). A variety of carbohydrates, including glucose, fructose, sucrose, and maltodextrins, have rather similar effects when given in a preload. They suppress later energy intake by an amount roughly equivalent to their caloric value, although the time course of the suppressive action may vary a little according to the rate at which the carbohydrate loads are metabolized.

In contrast, only a few studies have systematically investigated the extent to which dietary fat contributes to the satiating power of food. However, there is a widespread belief that high-fat diets are responsible for an elevated energy intake that in turn leads to weight gain through fat deposition. For example, researchers have shown that subjects undereat when forced to eat low-fat foods for three weeks, and overeat (relative to a balanced diet) when obliged to consume from an assortment of high-fat foods (e.g., Lissner, Levitsky, Strupp, Kackwarf, & Roe, 1987). These findings suggest that fat stimulates caloric intake. It is known that the fat content of food alters texture and palatability and may increase food acceptability. This factor, coupled with the high-energy density of fat, probably facilitates dietary excess within a meal or snack (by passive overconsumption). In addition, when subjects (lean or obese) consume large amounts of fat from a range of high-fat foods, this excessively large intake exerts only a weak braking action on subsequent eating (Blundell, Cotton, Lawton, & Burley, 1992). In other words, fat has a disproportionately weak action on satiety. Taken together, these findings show why diets high in fat can promote weight gain and lead to obesity. In addition, this relationship between nutrition and the expression of appetite confirms that the biopsychological system has only a weak defence against overconsumption (Figure 2).

MOTIVATION: ORDER AND DISORDER

Consideration of the relationship between nutrition and appetite illustrates clearly the interactive processes underlying the expression of the motivation to eat. The forces that impel and guide people to eat do not arise entirely internally, but are the result of mechanisms "under the skin" acting in concert with events in the environment. One of the most prominent of these environmental events is the type of food that people have available. In turn, this food has sensory and nutritional components. The sensory aspects of food (taste, smell, texture, mouth-feel) contribute to the perceived palatability (liking) of food, and this represents a hedonic quality. Together, the hedonic and nutritional components of food influence the pattern of the motivation to eat.

Of course, the emerging pattern of motivation arises from the processing of food by physiological and metabolic actions and by the events represented in the satiety cascade (Figure 4). The pattern of motivation takes the form of discrete episodes of behaviour (meals, snacks, etc.) along with oscillations in the strength of subjectively perceived hunger. As noted earlier, hunger is usually closely related to eating events. Consequently, there is a synchrony between the profile of hunger and the pattern of eating behaviour. In turn, this pattern of events is synchronized with peripheral physiological actions concerned with the handling of food in the body. A third level of events involves neural mechanisms in the brain that reflect physiological and behavioural happenings. It follows that the orderly expression of motivation involves a synchrony between the behavioural (and subjective) pattern, peripheral physiological events, and brain mechanisms (see Blundell, 1991, for a detailed account).

This well-synchronized control of motivation (expression of appetite) is an important factor in the maintenance of general health. One aspect of this synchrony involves the modulation of hunger in accordance with biological needs and environmental demands. In societies where food is plentiful, the relatively mild experience of hunger plays a biologically useful role in the orderly regulation of eating patterns. When food is scarce, however, the power of hunger can drive people to desperate deeds.

In addition, there are some clinical conditions that appear to reflect some disorder in the control of motivation. This occurs, for example, in extreme forms of dieting, periods of bingeing and fasting, and in the condition of bulimia nervosa (which often involves self-induced vomiting after food ingestion). These behavioural patterns create a de-synchrony among the behavioural, physiological, and neural levels. In addition, there is a disorderly relationship between the profile of hunger and the pattern of eating (Blundell & Hill, 1990). This labile or unregulated hunger reflects a pathology of appetite.

The view of appetite as the output of a biopsychological system indicates how the motivation to eat plays a natural role in maintaining the well-being and biological functioning of human beings (and animals). The system also indicates the role of hunger and its relationship to the expression of appetite. Given the complexity of the system, we should expect to find that appetite is influenced by many factors. This is certainly the case, but the potential complexity of these issues should not prevent us from comprehending the principles that regulate the form of this motivation.

FURTHER READING

Friedman, M. I., Tordoff, M. G., & Kare, M. R. (1991). *Appetite and nutrition*. New York: Marcel Dekker.

Hill, A. J., & Blundell, J. E. (1993). A practical guide to the measurement of eating behaviour and food intake. *International Journal of Obesity*.

LeMagnen, J. (1988). *Hunger*. Cambridge: Cambridge University Press.

Loge, A. W. (1991). *The psychology of eating and drinking* (2nd edn). New York: Freeman.

Shepherd, R. (1989). *Handbook of the psychophysiology of human eating*. Chichester: Wiley.

REFERENCES

Blundell, J. E. (1979). Hunger, appetite and satiety: Constructs in search of identities. In M. Turner (Ed.) *Nutrition and lifestyles* (pp. 21−42). London: Applied Science.

Blundell, J. E. (1981). Deep and surface structures: A qualitative approach to feeding. In L. A. Cioffi, W. P. T. James, & T. Van Itallie (Eds) *The body weight regulatory system: Normal and disturbed mechanisms* (pp. 73−82). New York: Raven.

Blundell, J. E. (1984). Serotonin and appetite. *Neuropharmacology, 23*, 1537−1551.

Blundell, J. E. (1991). Pharmacological approaches to appetite suppression. *Trends in Pharmacological Sciences, 12*, 147−157.

Blundell, J. E., & Hill, A. J. (1986). Biopsychological interactions underlying the study and treatment of obesity. In M. J. Christie & P. G. Mellet (Eds) *The psychosomatic approach: Contemporary practice of whole person care* (pp. 115−138). Chichester: Wiley.

Blundell, J. E., & Hill, A. J. (1990). Serotonin, eating disorders and the satiety cascade. In G. B. Cassano & H. S. Akiskal (Eds) *Serotonin-system-related syndromes (SRS): Psychopathological and therapeutic links* (pp. 125−129). London: Royal Society of Medicine.

Blundell, J. E., & Rogers, P. J. (1991). Hunger, hedonics and the control of satiation and satiety. In M. I. Friedman, M. G. Tordoff, & M. R. Kare (Eds) *Appetite and nutrition* (pp. 127–148). New York: Marcel Dekker.

Blundell, J. E., Rogers, P. J., & Hill, A. J. (1988). Uncoupling sweetness and calories: Methodological aspects of laboratory studies on appetite control. *Appetite, 11* (suppl. 1), 54–61.

Blundell, J. E., Cotton, J. R., Lawton, C. L., & Burley, V. J. (1992). Dietary fat and appetite control: Weak effects on satiation (within meals) and satiety (between meals). In D. J. Mela (Ed.) *Dietary fats: Determinants of preference, selection and consumption* (pp. 79–103). London: Elsevier.

Booth, D. A. (1972). Postabsorptively induced suppression of appetite and the energostatic control of feeding. *Physiology and Behavior, 9,* 199–202.

Booth, D. A. (1977). Satiety and appetite are conditioned reactions. *Psychosomatic Medicine, 39,* 76–81.

Bouchard, C. (1985). Inheritance of fat distribution and adipose tissue metabolism. In J. Vague, P. Bjorntorp, B. Guy-Grand, M. Rebuffe-Scrive, & P. Vague (Eds) *Metabolic complications of human obesities* (pp. 87–96). Amsterdam: Excerpta Medica.

Boyd Eaton, F., & Konner, M. (1985). Paleolithic nutrition: A consideration of its nature and current implications. *New England Journal of Medicine, 312,* 283–289.

De Castro, J. M., & Elmore, D. K. (1988). Subjective hunger relationships with meal patterns in the spontaneous feeding behavior of humans: Evidence for a causal connection. *Physiology and Behavior, 43,* 159–165.

Garcia, J., Hankins, W. G., & Rusiniak, K. W. (1974). Behavioral regulation of the milieu interne in man and rat. *Science, 185,* 24–31.

Keys, A., Brozek, J., Henschel, A., Mickelsen, O., & Taylor, H. L. (1950). *The biology of human starvation* (vol. 2). Minneapolis, MN: University of Minnesota Press.

Kissileff, H. R. (1984). Satiating efficiency and a strategy for conducting food loading experiments. *Neuroscience and Biobehavioral Reviews, 8,* 129–135.

Lissner, L., Levitsky, D. A., Strupp, B. J., Kackwarf, H., & Roe, D. A. (1987). Dietary fat and the regulation of energy intake in human subjects. *American Journal of Clinical Nutrition, 46,* 886–892.

Mattes, R. (1989). Hunger ratings are not a valid proxy measure of reported food intake in humans. *Appetite, 15,* 103–113.

Mei, N. (1985). Intestinal chemosensitivity. *Physiology Reviews, 65,* 211–237.

Monello, L. F., & Mayer, J. (1967). Hunger and satiety sensations in men, women, boys and girls. *American Journal of Clinical Nutrition, 20,* 253–261.

Reynolds, V. (1976). *The biology of human action*. San Francisco, CA: Freeman.

Richter, C. P. (1943). Total self-regulatory functions in animals and human beings. *Harvey Lecture Series, 38,* 63–103.

Rogers, P. J., Carlyle, J., Hill, A. J., & Blundell, J. E. (1988). Uncoupling sweetness and calories: Comparison of the effect of glucose and three intense sweeteners on hunger and food intake. *Physiology and Behavior, 43,* 547–552.

Rolls, B. J., Rowe, E. A., & Rolls, E. (1982). How sensory properties of foods affect human feeding behavior. *Physiology and Behavior, 29,* 409–417.

Royce, J. R. (1963). Factors as theoretical constructs. *American Psychologist, 18,* 522–528.

Van Itallie, T. B., & Vanderweele, D. A. (1981). The phenomenon of satiety. In P. Bjorntorp, M. Cairella, & A. N. Howard (Eds) *Recent advances in obesity research* (vol. 3, pp. 278–289). London: Libbey.

3

SOCIAL MOTIVATION

Russell G. Geen
University of Missouri, USA

Motivation refers, in a general sense, to processes involved in the initiation, direction, and energization of individual behaviour. The term *social motivation* refers to the activation of these processes by situations in which other people are in close contact with the individual. It is usually assumed that the social situation does not provide specific cues for the behaviour of the individual. Such topics as direct social influence, persuasion, conformity, and social reinforcement are not, therefore, considered to be part of social motivation.

HISTORICAL BACKGROUND

The study of social motivation was begun by Triplett (1898), who observed that sport bicyclists pedalled with greater speed when they rode in the company of other cyclists than they did when riding alone. Among possible causes for this effect, Triplett suggested that "another can . . . be the means of releasing or freeing nervous energy for [the individual] that he cannot of himself release" (p. 516). In the first experimental study of this "dynamogenic" phenomenon, Triplett showed that subjects performed a reel-cranking task more rapidly when accompanied by another person performing the same task than they had done in isolation. This study introduced to psychology the phenomenon of *social facilitation* of performance, in which the presence of others produces an increase in individual motivation. Triplett studied situations in which the other persons present performed a task in concert with the individual; these became known as *coaction* settings. In 1904 Meumann reported the first study in which social facilitation was achieved by a passive *audience* that merely observed the individual perform (Cottrell, 1972).

Several years later, Ringelmann reported a series of studies (which had actually been conducted prior to Triplett's research) in which the presence of others appeared to lead to a loss in motivation (Kravitz & Martin, 1986). Ringelmann showed that when people are added to a group engaged in a physical task like rope-pulling, the amount of force exerted per person decreases as the size of the group increases. Although Ringelmann thought that this effect was due chiefly to loss of coordination as the group grew in size, he conceded that loss of motivation could also be involved.

The earliest studies in social motivation, therefore, showed that under some conditions the presence of others leads to motivational gains whereas under other conditions it produces motivational decrements. Interest in motivational losses in social settings – the so-called "Ringelmann effect" – declined sharply in the decades immediately following the original reports, but investigations of social facilitation, involving both the coaction and audience paradigms, were conducted sporadically during that period. The findings from these studies were mixed, however, and tended to show that the presence of audiences or coactors facilitated performance or had the opposite effect – what I shall designate as *social inhibition* of performance – about equally often. Research was seriously hampered by a lack of theoretical formulations that could explain these contradictory effects with a single set of premises.

SOCIAL FACILITATION

The modern era of research on social facilitation began with a major theoretical paper by Zajonc (1965). Attempting to explain the mixed evidence from previous studies, Zajonc proposed that (1) the presence of others elicits a drive-like state of arousal, (2) drive multiplies with habit strength for all responses in a situation, increasing the probability of a dominant response relative to a subordinate one, and (3) the dominant response is more likely to be the correct one on easy tasks than on difficult ones. From this, Zajonc concluded that the presence of others leads to social facilitation of performance on easy or overlearned tasks, but to social inhibition of performance on difficult ones. This finding had been reported earlier by Allport (1924) but not explained in theoretical terms.

The decade following the appearance of Zajonc's paper yielded numerous experimental investigations of social facilitation, most of them animated by Zajonc's arguments. Some sought to test his viewpoint and others to challenge it with alternative explanations. In 1977 Geen and Gange reviewed this literature and concluded that at that time the most parsimonious explanation for both social facilitation and social inhibition was the drive-theoretical viewpoint. In the years since that review the situation has changed; such a confident conclusion of the primacy of drive theory is no longer warranted.

To understand the changes that have come about in conceptualizations of social facilitation, it is necessary to note that theoretical explanations have generally involved two sequential steps. The first is the impact of the presence of others on the individual, which places the individual in a state that mediates subsequent behaviour. The second is a process activated by that state that produces facilitation or inhibition of behaviour. Figure 1 illustrates these two processes as they were described by drive theorists: the presence of others elicits drive, which energizes responses. The outcome of this energization process is either an increment or a decrement in performance, depending

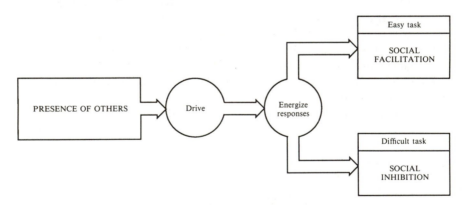

Figure 1 Schematic representation of drive theory of social facilitation. Rectangles containing terms in upper-case letters represent independent and dependent variables, respectively. Units labelled in upper-and-lower case letters represent hypothetical intervening variables. Of these, circles represent the two stages in the process described in the text

on task difficulty. Alternatives to the drive theoretical approach have involved departures from that theory at each of the two steps.

AROUSING EFFECTS OF SOCIAL PRESENCE

Evaluation apprehension

An early criticism of Zajonc's position concerned the nature of the social presence required for increased drive. Whereas Zajonc (1965) had concluded that the mere presence of others is sufficient to have this effect on the individual, certain investigators argued that the others must be regarded by the individual as potential judges and critics. The immediate precursor of increased drive is therefore thought to be anxiety or *evaluation apprehension*. For example, Cottrell and his associates (Cottrell, Wack, Sekerak, & Rittle, 1968) found that social facilitation of performance in the presence of others did not occur when the others were inattentive and unaware of what the individual was doing. Other studies have shown that audiences having a high social status exert a greater impact than audiences of lower status (e.g., Henchy & Glass, 1968), suggesting that the former may elicit stronger evaluation apprehension than the latter. In a study supporting this conclusion, Seta, Crisson, Seta, and Wang (1989) showed that the status of other persons present plays a role in generating arousal. Whereas the addition of high-status persons to an observing group leads to increased arousal in the observed individual, the addition of lower-status persons may actually reduce arousal by diminishing the overall level of anxiety over being evaluated.

Distraction/conflict

An alternative to both the mere presence and evaluation apprehension hypotheses is the idea that the presence of others distracts the individual from the task and thereby engenders response conflict. This conflict, in turn, causes increased arousal or drive. In a number of studies, Baron and his associates (e.g., Baron, Moore, & Sanders, 1978) have shown both that predicted social facilitation effects occur in audience settings and that the subjects in such settings are distracted by the observers. In many of these studies, it has been difficult to disentangle the effects of distraction from those of social facilitation, but in one experiment the two effects were successfully separated operationally. The results of this study (Groff, Baron, & Moore, 1983) clearly support the distraction/conflict hypothesis.

Uncertainty and social monitoring

In speculating on possible reasons that the "mere presence" of others generates increased arousal, Zajonc (1980) elaborated upon his earlier position by suggesting that socially generated drive may be the product of *uncertainty*. The presence of others implies the possibility of action on their part, and that the individual must always be alert to possible changes in the environment caused by the behaviour of others. Often such actions cannot be anticipated and therefore may elicit uncertainty.

Guerin and Innes (1982) have extended Zajonc's analysis to the process of *social monitoring*. Because others have the potential to create uncertainty by their presence, the individual must observe them periodically in an attempt to predict their actions. It is assumed that others who are present elicit less arousal when they can be observed and monitored than when they cannot. It is further predicted that the greatest amount of uncertainty is caused by others when they are nearby, attending to the individual, and outside the latter's range of monitoring. Guerin (1986) performed a meta-analysis of all studies in which the "mere presence" of others led to increased arousal (i.e., in which possible effects of evaluation apprehension were controlled). He concluded that in every such study the effects of the presence of others were attributable to either uncertainty or the absence of ability to monitor. In some the behaviour of the others was unpredictable whereas in others the others' behaviour was predictable but could not be monitored.

All of the proposed antecedents of socially induced arousal – evaluation apprehension, distraction-induced conflict, and uncertainty – have some empirical support. As has already been noted, separating the effects of evaluation apprehension from those of distraction has often been difficult. In the same way, a clear line between evaluation apprehension and uncertainty is difficult to draw: the person who is not being monitored may, without the individual's being able to discern, be evaluating the individual's performance.

ATTENTIONAL EFFECTS OF SOCIAL PRESENCE

Cognitive overload

Later formulations of social facilitation departed from the once-dominant view that drive constitutes the major intervening variable in the process. In an extension of his distraction/conflict model, Baron (1986) argued that the distraction from a task caused by being observed by others results in stimulus overload. This is a departure from the previously held idea that distraction engenders drive, because the consequences of cognitive overload are different from those of increased drive. Whereas drive energizes all responses in a situation (manifesting the second of the two steps in the social facilitation process outlined above), cognitive overload produces selectivity and narrowing of attention (Figure 2).

More specifically, Baron proposed that attentional conflict produced by distraction places demands on the person that may exceed the person's

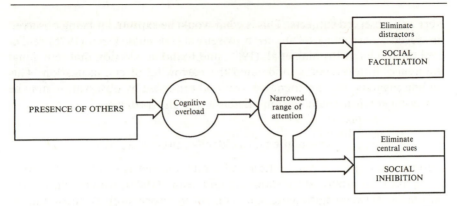

Figure 2 Schematic representation of cognitive overload theory of social facilitation. See legend to Figure 1 for explanation

capacity for attention. It is assumed that every person has a finite attentional capacity, and that as demands arise, the smaller is the spare capacity left over for such activities as problem solving. One result of overload is increased effort to pay attention, which can produce a momentary increase in arousal. The significance of this arousal does not lie in its energizing task-related responses, however, as drive theory would hold. Instead, it is a concomitant of effortful attention. The main functional response to cognitive overload is a narrowing of attention to a relatively narrow range of central cues, thereby reducing the load on the attentional system. Reduction in the range of cue utilization under such conditions has been described by several investigators (e.g., Easterbrook, 1959; Geen, 1980).

This reduction in the range of stimuli to which the person attends has effects on the performance of simple and complex tasks similar to those previously attributed to increased drive. Simple tasks require attention to a relatively small number of central cues, whereas complex tasks demand attention to a wide range of cues. Stimulus overload produces a narrowing in the range of cue utilization for both simple and complex tasks. When the task is simple, this narrowing terminates attention to irrelevant distractors, but when the task is complex, the same process leads to the elimination of important task-related information.

Only a few studies have examined the role of being observed on attentional processes. Bruning, Capage, Kozuh, Young, and Young (1968) found that being observed by the experimenter was associated with better performance by subjects who had been given additional irrelevant (and hence potentially distracting) information about their task, relative to the performance of subjects who were not observed. In addition, being observed was harmful to subjects given additional relevant information. Both findings suggest that being observed led subjects to be less influenced by the additional information than were non-observed subjects. This is what would be expected if being observed produced a narrowing of attention to central task cues. Geen (1976) replicated the results of Bruning et al. (1968) and found in addition that individual differences in test anxiety moderated the narrowing of cue utilization. This finding suggests that the cognitive overload produced by observation may be exacerbated when evaluation apprehension is also present.

Automatic and controlled processing

An approach to social facilitation and inhibition that is similar to the foregoing has been proposed by Manstead and Semin (1980), who emphasize the difference between automatic and controlled processing of information. Automatic processing develops with increasing familiarity with the task and a concomitant decreasing need for sustained attention. Once performance has become routine, attention is no longer required. Controlled processing is used when performance has not become routine and requires continuous attention to task demands. It follows from this that automatic processing is not limited by attentional capacity, whereas controlled processing is. Manstead and Semin (1980) propose that performance on novel or complex tasks, which require considerable controlled processing, is impaired by the presence of others, who make competing demands on attention. Performance on easy, familiar, or overlearned tasks, which are processed automatically, is not affected by such demands. Instead, the presence of others may prompt a focus of attention on otherwise ignored behavioural sequences and thereby bring about improved performance.

SELF-PRESENTATIONAL CONCERNS AND SOCIAL FACILITATION

The presence of others has effects on the individual that go beyond both arousal and cognitive overload by engaging and activating a need to present a desired or idealized self-image to others. Self-presentation motives have been shown to play a role in several studies. The findings of these studies are sometimes cited as evidence against the drive theoretical explanation of social facilitation, and it is true that they often report effects that cannot be accounted for by that approach. For example, Bond (1982) designed an experiment in which drive theory and self-presentation theory made directly opposite predictions and found that the latter accounted for the social facilitation effect. Other studies (reported below), while being less directly crucial in comparing the two theories, have adduced evidence that under some conditions the self-presentation theory can explain results that are inexplicable in terms of drive theory. Three approaches to social facilitation that employ the concepts of self-presentation have been proposed.

Self-awareness

Carver and Scheier (1981) have proposed that the effect of the presence of others increases the individual's sense of self-awareness, making him or her more cognizant of not only personal behaviour but also an ideal standard of performance for the task at hand. In keeping with their general theory of behaviour, in which action is generated to reduce or eliminate discrepancies between one's actual level of performance and a standard, Carver and Scheier propose further that the decision to undertake such action depends on the perceived probability of successful matching-to-standard. When the task is easy, and the probability of successfully matching the ideal is high, the person proceeds to complete the task; in this case, the presence of others, by bringing the real-ideal discrepancy into focus, therefore facilitates performance. However, when the task is difficult, the person is more likely to perceive the probability of success as too low and to give up. The presence of others, therefore, causes effort, and subsequent task performance, to cease or to become minimal (Figure 3).

Impression management

Another self-presentational approach to social facilitation is based on the premise that people strive to present the best possible appearance to others so that they may make a favourable impression. Observers or co-actors may not only motivate individuals to work hard at tasks but also exacerbate the person's sense of embarrassment when performance leads to failure. Such

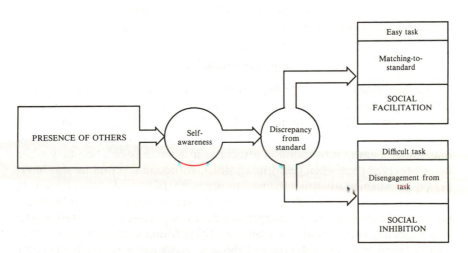

Figure 3 Schematic representation of self-awareness theory of social facilitation. See legend to Figure 1 for explanation

failure is less likely when the task is easy than when it is hard, so that the increased motivation may be sufficient to produce performance of high quality. Difficult tasks often result in failure, however, at least at the outset. Embarrassment evoked by such failure may cause stress and cognitive interference that disrupts subsequent performance. The previously cited study by Bond (1982) was conducted in the context of this approach.

Thus evaluation apprehension, which was earlier shown to be an antecedent of arousal, also plays an important role in presentation of the self. Baumeister (1982) makes this point in asserting that the desire to make a good impression is a fundamental motive and that fear of negative evaluation arises whenever the person has some concern over being able to present the self adequately.

Consistent with this line of reasoning, several studies have shown that when the person is subjected to an experience of failure just before performing a task (which should increase feelings of evaluation anxiety), subsequent performance before observers is poorer than it is when no prior failure is experienced (e.g., Seta & Hassan, 1980). Geen (1979) obtained similar findings among observed subjects who had first been exposed to failure, and in addition found that when a success experience preceded the task, performance among observed subjects was *superior* to that of subjects who performed the task without preliminary treatment. Because the task used by Geen was a difficult one, this finding goes against what would have been predicted from drive theory, but it is consistent with the self-presentational approach. In a subsequent study, Geen (1981) showed that subjects who are observed following success are more persistent at a second task than those who work alone, suggesting that self-presentation needs lead to greater motivation to succeed.

Response withholding

Evaluation apprehension arising from the presence of others can also influence performance by motivating the individual to refrain from behaving in ways that may be socially undesirable. This may have several effects. An early experiment in social facilitation by Matlin and Zajonc (1968) revealed that subjects gave more common associates in a word association task while being observed than when performing alone. Although this finding was interpreted as evidence for drive theory inasmuch as drive could have energized dominant verbal habits at the expense of subordinate ones, subsequent research suggests another interpretation. In replicating the Matlin and Zajonc study, Blank, Staff, and Shaver (1976) found that the major difference between observed subjects and those working alone was that the latter emitted a greater number of unusual and idiosyncratic associates than the former. The results were interpreted as indicating that observed subjects suppressed unusual responses in favour of more common ones in order to avoid looking strange to the observer.

Response suppression has also been demonstrated in a series of studies by Berger and his associates (Berger et al., 1981), who found that the presence of an audience motivates subjects to suppress overt practice (e.g., moving one's lips while reading, counting out loud) while performing a task. Because these devices assist learning, their suppression should inhibit performance on difficult tasks. Elimination of such overt practice on easy tasks may have the beneficial effect of compelling the person to use more symbolic processing, which should improve performance on such tasks. The upshot of all this is that if for any reason the person feels constrained to inhibit overt motoric practice, learning unfamiliar material will be hindered but learning familiar material will not. Berger further suggests that persons who are observed while learning will feel such constraints because of a cultural norm that discourages such overt activity. Thus the presence of an audience should facilitate performance on familiar tasks but inhibit performance on unfamiliar ones. In several experiments, Berger and his associates have found support for this hypothesis.

A third line of research that has linked the presence of an audience to response inhibition is constituted by several studies by Geen (1985; 1987) on the relationship of evaluation apprehension to passive avoidance. Briefly stated, the major hypothesis of this research is that when people are anxious in an evaluative situation and are also unable to leave the situation physically, they withhold or restrain responding in an effort to avoid making errors. If the presence of observers elicits evaluation apprehension, one reaction to audience settings may be cautiousness in responding, reflected in a low response rate. Furthermore, because complex and difficult tasks evoke more anxiety than simple ones, the greatest amount of response withholding should come on difficult tasks. This would lead to relatively poor performance, whereas on simple tasks the relatively moderate response withholding would have no such effect. Instead, a slightly slower response rate could facilitate greater attention to simple tasks because the person is not distracted by his or her own action, and this could lead to a slight facilitation of performance (Figure 4).

Geen (1985) found some support for this hypothesis in a study in which subjects who were high in test anxiety (as measured by a standard test anxiety scale) attempted to solve fewer anagrams while being watched by an evaluating experimenter than while either being observed in a non-evaluative way or while working alone. Subjects in the high anxiety-evaluated condition also reported higher levels of state anxiety than highly test anxious subjects in the other two conditions. In addition, the correlation between state anxiety and number of anagrams attempted was negative in every condition of the experiment and the highest negative correlation was found in the high anxiety-evaluated group. The results showed, therefore, that being observed by an

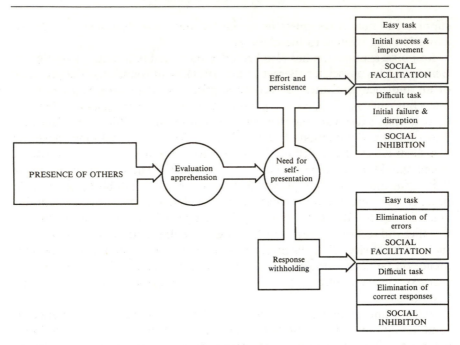

Figure 4 Schematic representation of impression management theory of social facilitation. See legend to Figure 1 for explanation

evaluator creates state anxiety, and that state anxiety produces a depressed rate of task-relevant responding.

In a second study of response withholding, Geen, Thomas, and Gammill (1988) tested the joint effect of observation and co-action on performance, following a hypothesis suggested by Geen (1980) that co-action effects should be greater when the experimenter is present and observing during the task. Subjects who performed with three co-actors while the experimenter was observing attempted fewer anagrams and reported higher levels of state anxiety than did subjects who performed under co-action conditions with the experimenter absent. When the experimenter was absent, no overall co-action effect was found, suggesting that the co-action effect was mediated by experimenter presence. Geen (1980) had argued that the presence of co-actors influences social facilitation by creating competition among the co-actors which, in turn, leads each subject to fear being outperformed by the others. If the experimenter, who is usually regarded as the purveyor of rewards and punishments, is present and evaluating each subject's performance, the evaluation apprehension in the situation is even higher. It is this heightened apprehension that leads to response inhibition and state anxiety in the co-action-experimenter present condition.

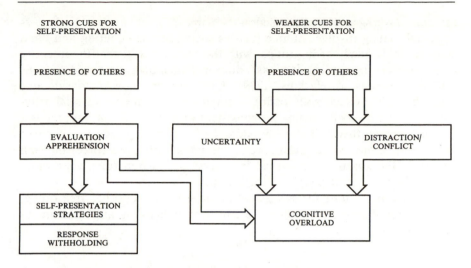

Figure 5   Overview of theories of social facilitation and inhibition
Source: Adapted from Geen, 1989

Conclusion

Geen (1989) has proposed a model of the processes involved in social facilitation that summarizes most of what has been covered in this discussion (see Figure 5). It is based on a few assumptions. First, all social situations contain some cues informing the person that he or she should strive to make a good self-presentation. Some situations contain strong cues, such as prior success (e.g., Geen, 1979) or tasks having the potential for embarrassment (e.g., Berger et al. 1981); other situations contain weaker cues. Second, when strong self-presentation cues are present, the person experiences a high level of evaluation apprehension, accompanied by behaviour calculated to protect the person from making a bad impression (i.e., strategic self-presentation and response withholding). Third, when self-presentation cues are weaker, the dominant response of the individual to the social presence will be uncertainty or distraction. These will contribute to cognitive overload. Evaluation apprehension may also lead to cognitive overload in addition to any self-presentational effects that it has. The effects of self-presentational concerns, response withholding, and cognitive overload on social facilitation or inhibition of performance have already been discussed (see Figure 4).

SOCIAL LOAFING

The phenomenon of apparent motivation loss in groups studied by Ringelmann (see above) was resurrected in the late 1970s by Latané and his associates, who gave the phenomenon the name of *social loafing*. Early tests of social loafing involved simple physical acts such as shouting and hand clapping individually or in groups, with the general result that the intensity of output per person declined as additional members were added (e.g., Latané, Williams, & Harkins, 1979). Later studies showed considerable generality in the effect, with loafing occurring in several non-physical activities. The data on social loafing are consistent with one of the major premises of social impact theory (Latané & Nida, 1980): when a person is a member of a group subjected to social forces, the impact of those forces on each person in the group is diminished in inverse proportion to, among other things, the number of people in the group.

Several explanations for social loafing have been proposed: free riding, equalization of perceived output, evaluation apprehension, and matching to standard.

"Free riding" and the "sucker" effect

One reason for a loss of individual motivation is what Kerr (1983) has called the *free rider* effect. This occurs when each member of a group perceives that there is a high probability that some other member of the group will solve the problem at hand and that the benefits from this person's performance will go to all members. Given this view of things, each person concludes that his or her output is dispensable and exerts little effort as a result. As the size of the group increases, the probability likewise increases that someone else in the group will solve the problem. The importance of individual effort therefore become less and less as the size of the group increases.

Related to this effect is that of equalizing what may be perceived to be an inequitable output. If subjects in groups expect their partners to become free riders, they may respond by loafing for the purpose of bringing equality of effort to what they perceived to be an inequitable situation. By doing this the subjects avoid looking like "suckers" who work hard for a group goal while those about them do not. In support of this idea, Jackson and Harkins (1985) found that subjects shouted more while alone than they did when in pairs (i.e., they loafed) only when they had no information concerning their partners' intended level of effort. When informed that the partner intended to expend either a high or a low effort, subjects matched their outputs to those of the partner.

Evaluation apprehension

Social loafing has also been explained as a normal response to tasks that are tiring, uninteresting, and otherwise not likely to engage the person's involvement. This argument rests on the assumption that the tasks commonly used in research on social loafing are boring and meaningless. People therefore try to avoid doing them, and will unless social constraints are implemented. Kerr and Bruun (1981) call this the "hide-in-the-crowd" explanation, indicating that group members provide a cover of anonymity for the unmotivated individual. This cover is usually facilitated in experiments on loafing by the usual practice of pooling the outputs of the group members. Making each person's output identifiable eliminates social loafing (Williams, Harkins, & Latané, 1981).

This finding introduces the possibility that subjects become apprehensive about being evaluated by the experimenter (as has already been demonstrated in research on social facilitation), and that this is why they do not loaf under non-anonymous conditions. Such is especially the case when subjects believe that their performance is being compared to that of their co-actors, so that they are effectively in competition with the others. This will be more likely to occur, moreover, when all of the persons in the group are performing the same task than when they are working on different tasks. Harkins and Jackson (1985) found support for this hypothesis by showing that social loafing was least likely to occur in a group when the outputs of the individuals were identifiable and when all subjects worked at the same task. Thus, the condition in which the highest level of evaluation apprehension was created was also the one in which the least loafing occurred.

If experiments on group performance involve tasks that engage the interest or concern of the individual, a necessary condition for social loafing is absent and the effect is not obtained (Brickner, Harkins, & Ostrom, 1986). Social loafing is, therefore, attributable not so much to a loss of motivation in the group setting as to an absence of motivation due to the nature of the task that becomes manifest in behaviour under group conditions. Evaluation apprehension in this setting causes the individual to suppress the preferred response – inactivity – in favour of more socially desirable behaviour. Viewed in this way, absence of social loafing appears to represent a special case of response withholding under conditions of evaluation anxiety quite similar to that shown in studies reviewed above.

Matching to standard

The third explanation of social loafing involves the concept of matching-to-standard. This explanation assumes that apprehension over the possibility of being evaluated by the experimenter causes the person to match a standard for performance set by the experimenter (and that this matching is avoided under conditions that allow social loafing). Several studies have shown in addition that even when cues signalling evaluation by the experimenter are not present, social loafing may be eliminated by the invocation of other salient standards to which the person's output can be compared. These standards need not be social. Harkins and Szymanski (1988), for example, found that merely reminding the persons in a group of a personal performance standard for the behaviour in question was sufficient to eliminate social loafing, and Harkins and Szymanski (1989) obtained the same result by reminding individuals of a group standard.

Conclusion

Social loafing, once thought to be the product of a loss in motivation under group conditions, now appears to be a form of avoidance behaviour prompted by uninteresting and non-involving tasks. It is reduced or eliminated by establishing conditions that either remove the anonymity of the persons involved or remind the persons of certain standards of behaviour pertinent to the activity. The idea that the introduction of social, personal, or group standards increases motivation is consistent with certain theoretical formulations pertaining to the self. For example, Breckler and Greenwald (1986) have proposed that individuals select their behaviours in order to secure a favourable self-image, to make a good impression on other people, and to live up to the standards of important reference groups. People foreswear social loafing in spite of low motivation for the task because of salient personal, social, and collective standards for behaviour. These three standards may, in turn, all be the products of a larger superordinate motive: the motive to be included in the social collective. To understand this, we must consider the motivational bases for evaluation apprehension, social anxiety, and self-presentation.

THE NEED FOR SOCIAL INCLUSION

Theory and research on both social facilitation and social loafing suggest that evaluation apprehension is an important motive for human behaviour in social settings. Each phenomenon may therefore be thought of as a manifestation of a more general influence of *social anxiety*, which has been defined as a state brought about by a person's being motivated to make a certain impression on others but doubting that this impression can be made (Schlenker & Leary, 1982). To avoid this state the person adopts various strategies of self-presentation and impression management in the hopes of creating a favourable impression and, as a consequence, of maintaining self-esteem. That is, the person adopts a course of action that enables him or her to overcome doubts about securing a desirable social outcome.

The impression management strategy in social facilitation, seen in such behaviour as trying harder to succeed in the presence of an audience following success than following failure (Geen, 1979; 1981), typifies such behaviour. The person appraises the social situation as one that threatens to be embarrassing should the person fail and, as a consequence, the person increases effort to avoid failure. Inhibiting socially undesirable responses in social settings may also be seen as behaviour calculated to avoid the possibility of making a bad impression and hence avoiding social anxiety. Suppressing a desire to loaf in a group during a boring task because of fear of exposure or of not meeting an internalized standard may also be interpreted as behaviour aimed at avoiding anxiety.

Why should the fear of making a bad impression be such a powerful motive for individual behaviour? One answer is that people may wish to make a good impression in order to avoid social rejection or exclusion. Humans have a strong need to be accepted by, and included within, society.

Fear of death

One reason that people need to be included within the collective may be that human culture, which society represents, provides a buffer against facing one's own vulnerability and mortality (Greenberg, Psyzczynski, & Solomon, 1986). Society provides a "cultural drama" that gives meaning to life and without which the person would experience existential dread. The person is therefore motivated to fulfil an approved role in that drama. Meeting cultural standards brings approval, social acceptance, and self-esteem; failing to meet those standards and social expectations invites rejection. Avoiding failure and suppressing socially undesirable action is only part of the motivational complex elicited by fear of death and non-being. The same motive also elicits positive pro-social behaviours aimed at enhancing and strengthening the authority of social customs and demands (e.g., Rosenblatt, Greenberg, Solomon, Psyzczynski, & Lyon, 1989).

Exclusion anxiety

A theory related to that of Greenberg and his associates has been proposed by Baumeister and Tice (1990), who place less emphasis on existential concerns and more on the potentially adaptive side of social anxiety. Social anxiety may serve as a warning signal that social disapproval will occur unless an ongoing course of action is modified. Any behaviour that might make the person seem unattractive or useless to the group could invite social exclusion and thereby elicit the warning signal. Anxiety therefore interrupts behaviour, focuses attention on what is being done wrong, and motivates the person to seek an alternative course of action.

Among these alternatives, as already noted, are acts that help the person avoid failure or other negative outcomes by controlling behaviour, becoming more motivated to do some things and to refrain from doing others. The phenomena of social facilitation and social loafing fall within this broad domain of behaviour. However, it is also possible that the person will resort to other courses of action and sample from a wide range of cognitive strategies demonstrated in research on the maintenance of self-esteem, such as self-handicapping, a self-serving attributional bias, excuse-making, or symbolic self-completion (Geen, 1991). Each strategy can be thought of as a process whereby the person attempts to escape blame or criticism from others for failure or other socially undesirable outcomes.

SUMMARY

A common thread that connects the problem of social facilitation with that of social loafing is the construct of evaluation apprehension. Situations that evoke this affective state can elicit a number of intervening processes that lead in turn to the improvement or inhibition of performance. Such situations can also eliminate tendencies toward social loafing that may be evoked in group settings by boring or uninvolving tasks. Evaluation apprehension, in turn, is a facet of social anxiety, a state called forth whenever the person wishes to make a good impression on others but fears that others' evaluations will be negative. Finally, social anxiety may be a product of a larger and more general motivational state based on a need for inclusion in the social collective and its corresponding fear of social exclusion. Social motivation may, therefore, be a manifestation of basic social processes that have adaptive and even existential consequences.

FURTHER READING

Baron, R. S. (1986). Distraction-conflict theory: Progress and problems. In L. Berkowitz (Ed.) *Advances in experimental social psychology* (vol. 19, pp. 1–40). New York: Academic Press.

Carver, C. S., & Scheier, M. F. (1981). The self-attention-induced feedback loop and social facilitation. *Journal of Experimental Social Psychology*, *17*, 545–568.

Geen, R. G. (1989). Alternative conceptions of social facilitation. In P. Paulus (Ed.) *The psychology of group influence* (2nd edn, pp. 15–51). Hillsdale, NJ: Lawrence Erlbaum.

Harkins, S. G. (1987). Social loafing and social facilitation. *Journal of Experimental Social Psychology*, *23*, 1–18.

REFERENCES

Allport, F. H. (1924). *Social psychology*. Boston, MA: Houghton Mifflin.

Baron, R. S. (1986). Distraction-conflict theory: Progress and problems. In L. Berkowitz (Ed.) *Advances in experimental social psychology* (vol. 19, pp. 1–40). New York: Academic Press.

Baron, R. S., Moore, D., & Sanders, G. S. (1978). Distraction as a source of drive in social facilitation research. *Journal of Personality and Social Psychology*, *36*, 816–824.

Baumeister, R. F. (1982). A self-presentational view of social phenomena. *Psychological Bulletin*, *91*, 3–26.

Baumeister, R. F., & Tice, D. M. (1990). Anxiety and social exclusion. *Journal of Social and Clinical Psychology*, *9*, 165–195.

Berger, S. M., Hampton, K. L., Carli, L. L., Grandmaison, P. S., Sadow, J. S., & Donath, C. (1981). Audience-induced inhibition of overt practice during learning. *Journal of Personality and Social Psychology*, *40*, 479–491.

Blank, T. D., Staff, I., & Shaver, P. (1976). Social facilitation of word associations: Further questions. *Journal of Personality and Social Psychology*, *34*, 725–733.

Bond, C. F. (1982). Social facilitation: A self-presentational view. *Journal of Personality and Social Psychology*, *42*, 1042–1050.

Breckler, S. J., & Greenwald, A. G. (1986). Motivational facets of the self. In R. M. Sorrentino & E. T. Higgins (Eds) *Handbook of motivation and cognition* (vol. 1, pp. 145–164). New York: Guilford.

Brickner, M. A., Harkins, S. G., & Ostrom, T. M. (1986). Effects of personal involvement: Thought-provoking implications for social loafing. *Journal of Personality and Social Psychology*, *51*, 763–769.

Bruning, J. L., Capage, J. E., Kozuh, J. F., Young, P. F., & Young, W. E. (1968). Socially induced drive and the range of cue utilization. *Journal of Personality and Social Psychology*, *9*, 242–244.

Carver, C. S., & Scheier, M. F. (1981). The self-attention-induced feedback loop and social facilitation. *Journal of Experimental Social Psychology*, *17*, 545–568.

Cottrell, N. B. (1972). Social facilitation. In C. G. McClintock (Ed.) *Experimental social psychology* (pp. 185–236). New York: Holt.

Cottrell, N. B., Wack, D. L., Sekerak, G. J., & Rittle, R. H. (1968). Social facilitation of dominant responses by the presence of an audience and the mere presence of others. *Journal of Personality and Social Psychology*, *9*, 245–250.

Easterbrook, J. A. (1959). The effect of emotion on cue utilization and organization of behavior. *Psychological Review*, *66*, 187–201.

Geen, R. G. (1976). Test anxiety, observation, and the range of cue utilization. *British Journal of Social and Clinical Psychology*, *15*, 253–259.

Geen, R. G. (1979). Effects of being observed on learning following success and failure experiences. *Motivation and Emotion*, *3*, 355–371.

Geen, R. G. (1980). Test anxiety and cue utilization. In I. G. Sarason (Ed.) *Test anxiety: Theory, research and applications* (pp. 43–61). Hillsdale, NJ: Lawrence Erlbaum.

Geen, R. G. (1981). Effects of being observed on persistence at an insoluble task. *British Journal of Social Psychology*, *20*, 211–216.

Geen, R. G. (1985). Evaluation apprehension and response withholding in solution of anagrams. *Personality and Individual Differences*, *6*, 293–298.

Geen, R. G. (1987). Test anxiety and behavioral avoidance. *Journal of Research in Personality*, *21*, 481–488.

Geen, R. G. (1989). Alternative conceptions of social facilitation. In P. Paulus (Ed.) *The psychology of group influence* (2nd edn, pp. 15–51). Hillsdale, NJ: Lawrence Erlbaum.

Geen, R. G. (1991). Social motivation. *Annual Review of Psychology*, *42*, 377–399.

Geen, R. G., & Gange, J. J. (1977). Drive theory of social facilitation: Twelve years of theory and research. *Psychological Bulletin*, *84*, 1267–1288.

Geen, R. G., Thomas, S. L., & Gammill, P. (1988). Effects of evaluation and coaction in state anxiety and anagram performance. *Personality and Individual Differences*, *6*, 293–298.

Greenberg, J., Psyzczynski, T., & Solomon, S. (1986). The causes and consequences of a need for self-esteem: A terror management theory. In R. F. Baumeister (Ed.) *Public self and private self* (pp. 189–212). New York: Springer-Verlag.

Groff, B. D., Baron, R. S., & Moore, D. S. (1983). Distraction, attentional conflict, and drivelike behavior. *Journal of Experimental Social Psychology*, *19*, 359–380.

Guerin, B. (1986). Mere presence effects in humans: A review. *Journal of Experimental Social Psychology*, *22*, 38–77.

Guerin, B., & Innes, J. M. (1982). Social facilitation and social monitoring: A new look at Zajonc's mere presence hypothesis. *British Journal of Social Psychology*, *21*, 7–18.

Harkins, S. G., & Jackson, J. M. (1985). The role of evaluation in eliminating social loafing. *Personality and Social Psychology Bulletin*, *11*, 456–465.

Harkins, S. G., & Szymanski, K. (1988). Social loafing and self-evaluation with an objective standard. *Journal of Experimental Social Psychology*, *24*, 354–365.

Harkins, S. G., & Szymanski, K. (1989). Social loafing and group evaluation. *Journal of Personality and Social Psychology*, *56*, 934–941.

Henchy, T., & Glass, D. C. (1968). Evaluation apprehension and the social facilitation of dominant and subordinate responses. *Journal of Personality and Social Psychology*, *10*, 446–454.

Jackson, J. M., & Harkins, S. G. (1985). Equity in effort: An explanation of the social loafing effect. *Journal of Personality and Social Psychology*, *49*, 1199–1206.

Kerr, N. L. (1983). Motivation losses in small groups: A social dilemma analysis. *Journal of Personality and Social Psychology*, *45*, 819–828.

Kerr, N. L., & Bruun, S. E. (1981). Ringelmann revisited: Alternative explanations for the social loafing effect. *Personality and Social Psychology Bulletin*, *7*, 224–231.

Kravitz, D., & Martin, B. (1986). Ringelmann rediscovered: The original article. *Journal of Personality and Social Psychology*, *50*, 936–941.

Latané, B., & Nida, S. (1980). Social impact theory and group influence: A social engineering perspective. In P. Paulus (Ed.) *The psychology of group influence* (1st edn, pp. 3–34). Hillsdale, NJ: Lawrence Erlbaum.

Latané, B., Williams, K., & Harkins, S. G. (1979). Many hands make light the work: The causes and consequences of social loafing. *Journal of Personality and Social Psychology*, *37*, 822–832.

Manstead, A. S. R., & Semin, G. (1980). Social facilitation effects: Mere enhancement of dominant responses? *British Journal of Social and Clinical Psychology*, *19*, 119–136.

Matlin, M. W., & Zajonc, R. B. (1968). Social facilitation of word associations. *Journal of Personality and Social Psychology*, *10*, 435–460.

Rosenblatt, A., Greenberg, J., Solomon, S., Psyzczynski, T., & Lyon, D. (1989). Evidence for terror management theory: I. The effects of mortality salience on reactions to those who violate or uphold cultural values. *Journal of Personality and Social Psychology*, *57*, 681–690.

Schlenker, B. R., & Leary, M. R. (1982). Social anxiety and self-presentation: A conceptualization and model. *Psychological Bulletin*, *92*, 641–669.

Seta, J. J., & Hassan, R. K. (1980). Awareness of prior success or failure: A critical factor in task performance. *Journal of Personality and Social Psychology*, *39*, 70–76.

Seta, J. J., Crisson, J. E., Seta, C. E., & Wang, M. A. (1989). Task performance and perceptions of anxiety: Averaging and summation in an evaluative setting. *Journal of Personality and Social Psychology*, *56*, 387–396.

Triplett, N. (1898). The dynamogenic factors in pacemaking and competition. *American Journal of Psychology*, *9*, 507–533.

Williams, K., Harkins, S. G., & Latané, B. (1981). Identifiability as a deterrent to social loafing: Two cheering experiments. *Journal of Personality and Social Psychology*, *40*, 303–311.

Zajonc, R. B. (1965). Social facilitation. *Science*, *149*, 269–274.

Zajonc, R. B. (1980). Compresence. In P. Paulus (Ed.) *Psychology of group influence* (1st edn, pp. 35–60). Hillsdale, NJ: Lawrence Erlbaum.

4

SEXUAL MOTIVATION AND BEHAVIOUR

John Bancroft

MRC Reproductive Biology Unit, Edinburgh, Scotland

Reproduction by sexual means is a universal characteristic of multicellular living organisms. In bringing the male and female germ cells together, nature has evolved an extraordinarily rich variety of biological strategies. In plants, intermediate devices are often employed – insects, water, wind, and so on. In the animal kingdom some specific pattern of behavioural interaction of male and female is nearly always involved.

In most animal species, this process is dangerous; vigilance is reduced and vulnerability to predators increased. As a consequence, reproductive behaviour is restricted to whatever is needed for optimum reproductive consequences, timed to occur during the fertile phase of the female's reproductive cycle. Sexual behaviour has therefore evolved to be under control of the same hormones that determine other aspects of the reproductive process, in particular the gonadal steroid hormones testosterone, oestradiol, and progesterone.

In mammals, the pattern of hormonal control of the female's sexual behaviour varies across species. Males are more consistent, with testosterone being necessary for both adequate sexual behaviour and male fertility in virtually all species. However, sexual behaviour is by no means under absolute control of such hormones. Genetic influences are important; some individuals are more responsive than others to these hormonal effects on behaviour. Learning is also crucial; in most mammalian species that have been studied, disruption of normal relationships between the young animal and the mother and/or the peer group results in impairment of later sexual behaviour, particularly in the male, which, in primates, may be quite intractable (Larsson, 1978).

PRIMATE SEXUALITY: THE COMPARATIVE APPROACH

Darwin (1871) described two types of sexual selection: *intrasexual*, best exemplified by competition between males for access to the female, and *intersexual*, when characteristics of one gender increase the likelihood of being accepted or chosen as a mate by the other. These two types of selection often interact, as when the female is most attracted to the male who dominates the male–male competition.

Whatever the process of mate selection, the investment in parenting differs for the male and the female. There is no biological constraint on the number of offspring fathered by a male; there are clear constraints on the female, whether she has only one partner or many. Such contrasts contribute to the evolution of male–female differences in behavioural aptitudes.

We find that in any particular species of mammal, the pattern of mating and adaptation to the environment interact to have powerful influences on social structure. In those species where male–male competition is pre-eminent, the associated social structure will depend on the needs for environmental adaptation. The orang-utan, for example, lives in an environment which, in terms of food supply, can sustain only the occasional animal. Male–male competition determines which male occupies a particular territory, usually a quite extensive area. A small number of females may also inhabit the same territory but keep away from the male, usually for long periods of lactational infertility, making themselves available to the male only when they are in heat. The gorilla, by contrast, lives among relatively abundant food supply and the successful male keeps a harem of females to himself, driving male offspring away when they approach maturity and maintaining his position until he succumbs to a younger more powerful male.

The chimpanzee has evolved to live in social groups in which the males cooperate to protect the group from external threats. The mating pattern is very different again (Tutin, 1980); when a female in the group is in heat (or oestrus), all or most of the males will mate with her. This pattern serves to reduce male–male competition and foster group cohesiveness. Its non-reproductive function is also aided by the relatively long period of oestrus, which encourages sexual activity for more than one-third of the female's reproductive cycle and is much longer than that required for reproductive purposes.

In the case of the gorilla (and orang-utan), the *polygynous* pattern of mating is associated with marked sexual dimorphism, the larger male being most successful in gaining access and winning the attraction of the female (the male is approximately twice the size of the female). The male chimpanzee is only slightly larger than the female, perhaps reflecting his defensive role in the group. The chimp's pattern of mating, relatively unusual among primates, is *promiscuous*, and characterized by a greater capacity for sperm production. The male gorilla ensures his reproductive success by his bodily size and strength; the chimpanzee by the number of ejaculations and sperm that he can produce during frequent mating. This is reflected in a high testis–body weight ratio, much higher in the chimpanzee than in the gorilla (Short, 1981).

Primates who show monogamous mating patterns, and who live in family groups (e.g., the gibbon or marmoset) show no sexual dimorphism and relatively low testis–body weight ratios. In such monogamous family groups sexual interaction between the maturing offspring and the parents is not tolerated. The integrity of the family group is maintained by socially induced delay of puberty and the driving away of the offspring once puberty is reached.

This variety of socio-sexual structure is also reflected in the level of sexual activity of the male and/or female that characterizes a species. The male orang-utan is relatively highly sexed and will mate with any female he comes across, whether she is receptive or not. That is why the female keeps out of his way until she is in heat. The male gorilla, by comparison, is relatively uninterested in sex and requires the particular stimulation of the oestrous female to activate his behaviour. This depends not only on the female's attractiveness to him when in heat, but also on her behaviour in soliciting his interest. Thus one can see that a female gorilla, or a female orang-utan, whose behaviour is not influenced appropriately by the hormonal changes that accompany her fertile period, is unlikely to reproduce herself.

This comparison of three of the Great Apes, who in evolutionary and genetic terms are probably among the closest relatives of the human primate, illustrates the three components of female sexuality, first defined by Beach

(1976), that have dominated much of the biological investigation of animal sexual behaviour: first, *attractiveness*, shown by the female chimp in heat who emits hormonally determined signals, both olfactory and visual (the extraordinary and very obvious enlargement of her external genitalia), which sexually excite the males in the group; second, *proceptivity*, the active behaviour of the female that elicits a sexual response from the male, as shown by the female gorilla in oestrus or, in a somewhat different way, by the female orang-utan, who when in oestrus makes herself available to the male; and third, *receptivity*, the acceptance by the female of the male's advance and attempted mounting.

This analysis has facilitated our understanding of the role of hormones in the sexual behaviour of female primates as well as other mammals. In most species oestrogens play a crucial role in attractiveness (though learning, by the male, of the sexual significance of olfactory or visual cues may also be of importance), and perhaps particularly in the sub-primate mammals, in receptivity. Testosterone, possibly in combination with oestrogens, plays an important role in female proceptivity (Dixson, 1983). Interestingly, investigation of male sexuality has been somewhat more simplistic – little attention has been given to the notion of attractiveness or receptivity of the male. In a somewhat chauvinistic way, the male is seen as simply "proceptive".

This "three species" comparison also shows us that sexuality can evolve to serve non-reproductive purposes to a degree that is not simply determined by the level of evolutionary complexity. The role of sexual behaviour in the social organization of the chimpanzee is striking. By comparison, sex has little non-reproductive purpose for the gorilla. But in other primate species we see the function of sexual intimacy in affectional bonding between animals, which has relevance to parental relationships as well as to other aspects of the social process.

The type of analysis so far presented is relatively uncontroversial when confined to non-humans. There are, of course, many differences to be found among non-human species in the biological mechanisms that influence sexual behaviour. But there are also many commonalities. It would make little sense to assume that the biological mechanisms involved in human sexuality are unique to humans, any more than are mechanisms involved in eating behaviour, or aggression, or cardiovascular physiology. It would also be unwise to assume that social determinants of non-human primate behaviour are irrelevant to the human. On the other hand, there are crucial features of the human situation that are uniquely human. The challenge is to place those features and mechanisms into perspective.

Nevertheless, the use of this cross-species comparative approach to further our understanding of the human situation tends to elicit a polarity of attitudes which, while of general relevance, is particularly marked when our sexuality and issues of gender are concerned. This is the contrast between those who seek to explain human behaviour in either predominantly biological or predominantly sociological terms. For many thinking people such polemic is futile, the importance of both biological and sociological determinants are obvious; the intellectual challenge is to understand how they interact. But the polemic continues almost unabated. An analysis of its origins is beyond the scope of this chapter, although the political implications are among the most relevant. Emphasis on the "biological imperative" reinforces acceptance of the status quo, which is of particular relevance to the position of women in our society. Hence, notions of biological determination of gender differences are particularly contentious and many feminist thinkers are intolerant of such explanations. Emphasis on social determination reinforces the aspirations of those who seek social change, whether or not such change is facilitated by such a view.

In a multi-authored volume (Geer & O'Donohue, 1987), a variety of theoretical approaches to understanding human sexuality was presented. These included sociological approaches such as scripting theory, feminist psychology, cognitive psychology, psychoanalysis, learning theory, anthropology and the evolutionary approach. While the interest and relevance of most of these approaches is apparent, what is intriguing is the extent to which some of the proponents regard their explanatory systems as sufficient. In contemplating the fundamental complexity of sexuality, especially of the human, one is reminded of the blind men and the elephant. We can obtain a variety of views of this complexity, each of which has its own validity and heuristic value, but which is inevitably incomplete. The goal should be to establish, not the real or correct explanation of human sexual behaviour, but rather a way of looking at it that serves a useful purpose. The most appropriate view will therefore vary according to that purpose. Educationalists may find an explanatory model emphasizing sociological and/or learning mechanisms more helpful than one emphasizing the biological. The feminist, concerned with improving the status of women in society, will need to emphasize the extent to which societal expectations of male sexual behaviour involve dominance over or exploitation of women. The clinician or professional, seeking to help those with problems in their sexual lives, requires a psychosomatic approach to understanding how psychological processes, and their social influences, interact with physiological mechanisms. It is from this background that this chapter has been written, attempting the difficult task of integrating sociological, psychological, and biological mechanisms (Bancroft, 1989).

HUMAN SEXUALITY

In the process of building our integrated view of human sexuality we can usefully consider two broad dimensions, the functions that sexual behaviour serves, and the mechanisms involved in implementing those functions.

The functions of sex

Although for most mammalian species the non-reproductive functions of sex are limited, we have already seen how in some primates they are more extensive, and for most humans they have a pervasive influence. Apart from reproduction we therefore have to consider the following:

Pleasure

Perhaps the primary, or most basic, reinforcer of sexual behaviour is the pleasure that can be experienced, a combination of sensual pleasure and the uniquely sexual pleasure associated with orgasm.

Pair-bonding and fostering intimacy

The vulnerability of being actively sexual is relevant to this function. In most species, as mentioned earlier, the dangers are physical, but for humans they are predominantly psychological. It can be argued that exposing oneself in this way in a sexual relationship, and finding oneself safe in the process, provides a particularly powerful form of bonding between two people. This is the essence of sexual intimacy. Experiencing and giving pleasure no doubt contribute to this process, but they may be less crucial to bonding than the experience of emotional security that is engendered. It is for this reason that the bonding effect of sexuality within a relationship is so readily threatened by sexual involvement outside the relationship.

Asserting masculinity or femininity

The issue of gender identity – how we feel about ourselves as male or female, and how we express that identity as behaviour – is a uniquely human issue deriving from our use of language and the consequent need to label and categorize various aspects of ourselves, others, and our environment (Money & Ehrhardt, 1972). During childhood, sexuality is relatively unimportant to our gender identity; pre-pubertal boys and girls establish their sense of gender in terms of their non-sexual interests, activities, and peer group relationships. Following puberty, when their bodies begin secondary sexual development, and their hormonal and social milieu change, sexuality becomes important. How attractive or effective one is in sexual terms becomes an important reinforcer of one's sense of gender, among other things. Much of early adolescent sexuality can be understood in this way. However, throughout our lives, particularly at times when our gender identity is threatened in other ways (e.g., a woman having to undergo a hysterectomy, a man being made redundant, the effects of ageing), we may use our sexuality for this purpose.

Bolstering self-esteem

Feeling sexually attractive to others, or succeeding in one's sexual endeavours, may generally improve our self-esteem (and conversely, in the face of sexual failure, lower it).

Achieving power or dominance

The "power" of sexuality tends to be regarded as an aspect of masculinity, with the male, for both social and physical reasons, typically being in a position of dominance. Sex can be used to control relationships, however, by both men and women, and is often an important aspect of the dynamics of a relationship. Power may be exerted by controlling access to sexual interaction, or determining the form that a sexual encounter takes. While in the clinical context it is most usual to encounter this aspect within an established relationship, it is also an important and interesting aspect of early "courtship" behaviour. Whereas women have legitimate reasons for fearing the abuse of power by men in sexual interaction, the extent to which women control normal sexual exchanges, determining when an interaction can progress to the next stage, is perhaps underestimated and under-researched. Perper (1985) studied this aspect of male–female interaction in the social context of "singles bars".

Expressing hostility

An important aspect of the "dominance" issue of male–female sexual interaction is the use of sexuality to express hostility. This is of most relevance to the problem of rape and sexual assault. Whereas many instances of sexual assault or coercive sex can be seen as an extension of dominance or power, usually by the male over the female, there are also instances when the sexual assault can be understood as an expression of anger, either against the individual woman, or against the woman as a representative of other women, or against the man whose property the assaulted woman is seen to be. This latter pattern is common in interracial rape (e.g., the black man raping the white woman) or rape during wartime (Brownmiller, 1975). There is much controversy about the extent to which rape should be understood as either an act of aggression or a sexual act. It is likely that, to understand many cases of rape and sexual assault, we shall need to understand how aggression and sexual arousal can interact (see below).

Reducing anxiety or tension

The reduction in arousal that typically follows orgasm may be used as a device to reduce anxiety or tension. While this is an occasional function for most people, it is most likely to become established as an habitual pattern when solitary masturbation is the main sexual outlet. In such circumstances, masturbation may increase in frequency when anxiety or tension is high.

Risk taking

For some individuals, taking risks is a form of excitement that they seek. Sexual interaction provides a variety of risks, ranging from the relatively benign, such as being found out, to the serious, such as pregnancy or sexually transmitted disease.

Material gain

Offering oneself as a sexual partner for payment or other material benefits is a well-established aspect of human sexuality, as well as being evident among primates. Prostitution, the institutionalized form of such sexuality, has been established in most human societies. The social function of prostitution, that is, the extent to which it serves the needs of a society, has been an issue of considerable debate at various times. Thus when there was a moral outrage against the level of prostitution and its consequences towards the end of the nineteenth century, the social benefits were often stressed implicitly if not explicitly, by those who wished to maintain the status quo (Davenport-Hines, 1990).

The mechanisms of human sexuality

Given the variety of functions that have been considered, what is it that endows an experience with a specifically sexual quality? Is it, as some sociological theorists would have us believe, mainly a question of whether the experience is labelled as sexual in the social context? Or are there intrinsically sexual characteristics, and if so what are they?

We can draw a useful parallel with eating behaviour. A hungry person experiences a subjective state we call appetite which motivates him or her to obtain food, focusing attention on that goal. The subjective state is accompanied by and partly consists of various physiological changes, many of which are in preparation for food intake. Both biochemical processes, such as hypoglycaemia, and psychological processes, such as thinking about food, are involved. We learn to feel hungry at certain times and in certain situations. Our appetite is increased by the sight or smell of food, and we learn to like certain foods more than others. As with sex, a variety of functions other than nutrition, some social, are met by the varieties of eating behaviour.

In the sexual context, what we experience as sexual appetite, or sexual desire, and what may subsequently become a state of sexual arousal, is also a complex interaction between cognitive processes, neurophysiological and biochemical mechanisms, and mood. How we behave in such circumstances will reflect the "scripts" that our social group has provided us. We can therefore view this complex interactive situation through these various "windows" and consider (1) neurophysiological arousability, (2) cognitive processes, (3) mood and emotional states, and (4) social influences or "scripts" for sexual action.

Neurophysiological arousability

The increase in central arousal or alertness that typically occurs when responding to a sexual stimulus focuses attention on the stimulus, and is accompanied by a range of physiological responses particularly involving the genitalia – penile erection in the male and genital tumescence and lubrication in the female. Orgasm, the culmination of this arousal process, is a uniquely sexual phenomenon, about which little is known (Bancroft, 1989). There are important sex differences; the frequency of orgasm (and ejaculation) in the male is limited by a "refractory period" of unarousability, which is relatively short in the adolescent but progressively lengthens as the man gets older. The frequency of orgasm in women is not restricted in the same way, perhaps because the reproductive consequences of frequent orgasms in the female would be unimportant, whereas in the male, infertility would result.

The localization of these various "sexual" functions within the central nervous system (CNS), at least in lower animals, is becoming established. The hypothalamus and other parts of the limbic system are important. The universality of such mechanisms across species is well illustrated by the function of the medial preoptic area of the hypothalamus. Lesions of this area result in deficits in sexual response in virtually all mammalian species that have been studied. The deficits are complex; they do not impair motivation for sexual interaction (a lesioned primate, for example, may continue to masturbate), but result in disruption of the complex motor and communicative responses that normally enable the animal to copulate with a mate (Hart & Leedy, 1985).

Central mechanisms are involved in *information processing*, that is, the recognition of a potentially sexual situation or partner, *genital responses*, and the complex pattern of motor behaviour and interaction with a sexual partner that results in *copulation and orgasm*. It is reasonable to assume, from the evidence that we have so far, that many of these neurophysiological mechanisms are involved in the sexual responses of the human, though how those responses are expressed and experienced will obviously be shaped by the uniquely human aspects of the information processing (Everitt & Bancroft, 1991).

Animal studies have shown that the neurotransmitters involved in the control of sexual behaviour are also involved in many aspects of brain function and are widely distributed in the CNS. By contrast, reproductive hormones such as testosterone and oestradiol have receptors that are more restricted in their distribution, located in areas involved in sexual responses and other brain mechanisms essential for reproduction. It is the interaction of the neurotransmitters with the hormones in specific brain areas that is crucial for many aspects of sexual response and behaviour.

The role of hormones: the male

The principal androgenic hormone in the male, testosterone, has a clear and fundamental role in the sexuality and fertility of men, as well as that of the male in most mammalian species (Bancroft, 1988). Increasing levels of testosterone in early adolescence are accompanied not only by development of secondary sexual characteristics, such as growth of the penis, sexual hair, and the onset of spermatogenesis, but also by increased sexual arousability, as shown by spontaneous erections during sleep and at other times. In one study, the sexual interest of the early adolescent boy, and his likelihood of masturbating and engaging in sexual interactions, were correlated more strongly with his level of free (i.e., biologically active) testosterone than with his stage of pubertal development (Udry, Billy, Morris, Groff, & Raj, 1985). A deficiency of testosterone in adult men is typically associated with a lack of sexual interest or desire, which can be improved by hormone replacement. The effects of testosterone on erectile function are more complex. Spontaneous erections, such as those that occur during sleep, are testosterone-dependent, and are impaired in states of hormone deficiency. By contrast, erections in response to visual erotic stimuli are relatively unaffected by testosterone lack, suggesting that there are aspects of sexual responsiveness in men that are testosterone-dependent, and others that are not. The erectile response to erotic imagery or fantasy may come into the hormone-dependent category, though the evidence is less clear. Testosterone is also necessary for normal spermatogenesis, and the hypogonadal man will be infertile. While seminal emission is testosterone-dependent, it is not yet clear whether this is the case for orgasm per se.

Testosterone, therefore, is necessary for normal sexual interest in men, but it is not sufficient. The considerable variation in the level of sexual interest among men cannot be explained in terms of variation in testosterone level, though genetic differences in the behavioural responsiveness to hormones may contribute. Other factors, not as yet understood, must contribute to an individual's constitutional level of sexual responsiveness.

The role of hormones: the female

Do women show a menstrual-cycle-related pattern of sexual interest or responsiveness comparable to the oestrus of most primates? In particular, are they more sexually interested or responsive, or attractive to their partners, around the time that they ovulate? The evidence remains inconclusive. The various studies that have relied on women's retrospective recall have found that a mid-cycle peak in sexuality is the least common pattern, women being more likely to report their peaks postmenstrually, premenstrually, or even during menstruation, or to be unaware of any particular cyclical pattern. The few studies in which hormonal changes have been measured in parallel with behaviour have produced conflicting results. Thus in some studies, peaks of sexuality have been postmenstrual (during the mid-follicular phase) rather than periovulatory (Bancroft, 1989). Others have shown evidence of a mid-cycle peak, the most convincing coming from a study of newly married African women, who showed peaks of coital activity around ovulation (Hedricks, Piccinino, Urdry, & Chimbia, 1987). One possible explanation for this variability is that the behavioural effect of the reproductive hormones will depend on the social and reproductive circumstances. In other words, if a woman is seeking pregnancy, as a young African woman is likely to be at the start of her marriage, then the behavioural effects of the periovulatory hormones may be interpreted differently, leading to desire for sexual intercourse. If fertility is not the goal, the effects may have a different significance. This implies an interaction between hormonal and cognitive processes, influenced by societal expectations. This would also be consistent with hormones having a different impact on the sexuality of women at different stages of their life cycle.

The interaction between mood and sexuality is also important. In one study one-third of the variance in sexual interest through the menstrual cycle was attributable to variations in well-being (Sanders, Warner, Backström, & Bancroft, 1983). Thus in women who experience noticeable changes in well-being through the cycle, peaks of sexual interest will be more likely at times when well-being is highest (e.g., postmenstrually).

Oestradiol, which is crucial to oestrus in many species, shows a very uncertain relationship to the sexuality of women, apart from its unequivocal role in the normal lubrication response of the vaginal wall to sexual stimulation. This latter effect is important for many post-menopausal women whose oestradiol levels have fallen. Testosterone is normally present in the circulation of women in approximately one-tenth of the quantity found in men, with about 50 per cent coming from the ovaries and 50 per cent from the adrenals. Its ovarian source varies cyclically, resulting in maximum levels around mid-cycle. This androgen appears to be relevant to sexual interest in women, as in men, though the evidence is much less consistent. The most convincing evidence comes from hormone replacement for women following the removal of their ovaries (Sherwin, 1991). However, such positive effects on sexuality involve supraphysiological levels of hormone. It is more difficult to demonstrate a relationship between sexuality and testosterone levels that vary within the woman's physiologically normal range.

In so far as testosterone is important for female sexuality, we are left with an intriguing riddle. It is often assumed that during the early organizing stages of our development, mainly prenatally, the relevant target organs of the male are sensitized to testosterone so that later, when androgens rise at puberty, the testosterone activates secondary sexual development, and sexual responsiveness, along male lines. By implication the female is less responsive to testosterone. But if women are responsive to testosterone, then even with the supraphysiological amounts referred to above, they are responding to levels which, in the male, would be in the hypogonadal range. This suggests that males are *less* sensitive to the behavioural effects of androgens than females, perhaps permitting them to be exposed to the much higher levels of androgens that are necessary for male muscular development and growth. If this is the case, then the initial exposure of the male foetus to consistently high levels of androgens must *de*sensitize the target cells in the brain. Females by comparison will be exposed to both lower and more variable levels of androgens during early development, resulting in more variable levels of target organ sensitivity. This offers one theoretical explanation for the apparently greater variability among women in the importance of testosterone for their sexuality.

Other explanations are worth considering. Given the pattern of sexual behaviour in human relationships, where frequency of sexual intercourse is greater than that required for optimum fertility, and the uncertain evidence of an oestrus in relation to the woman's ovarian cycle, it would be less important in terms of reproduction whether or not a woman responded behaviourally to her reproductive hormones. By contrast, for the man, for whom both fertility and sexual interest are clearly dependent on testosterone, any lack of responsiveness to testosterone would reduce his likelihood of reproducing himself. It is therefore possible that women have evolved to be genetically more variable than men in their behavioural responsiveness to reproductive hormones.

In general, we see more evidence that social influences are important to the sexuality of women than of men. Whether this is because the hormonal effects in women are generally weaker, or whether there are other explanations, is not yet clear.

Cognitive processes

Information processing is no less important for the sexuality of the rat than for that of the human. The situation has to be appraised, the availability of a suitable mate determined and the interaction with the mate negotiated. For the human, however, this information processing involves the appraisal of "meaning", and the repercussions of such meaning add a higher level of complexity.

Thus the sexuality of a situation, as perceived, will be susceptible to the full weight of human learning and the "social scripts" for sexual action, which we shall consider further below. At a more fundamental level of cognitive function, we need to consider the extent to which the individual is focusing attention not only on the sexual stimulus, but also on the physiological responses to it. Thus, if there is no distraction, there will be an escalation in which, confronted with a potentially sexual stimulus, the recognition of the response as sexual will lead to further response and associated arousal (Dekker & Everaerd, 1988). This process, it should be said, will not be independent of the neurophysiological substrate considered above. In a hypogonadal man, for example, whose arousability is impaired by testosterone deficiency, this process will be limited.

The importance of the cognitive component involves both the scope for altered meaning that it permits (a stimulus that is potentially sexual may be interpreted as non-sexual or even threatening) and the scope for distraction by other types of information processing that interfere with this escalating feedback process. There is now a substantial body of experimental evidence indicating how distracting stimuli impair the erotic response to a sexual stimulus (Cranston-Cuebas & Barlow, 1990). Interestingly, men can be more readily distracted from the erotic effects of auditory stimuli than of visual stimuli; women are distracted equally from both types of erotic stimuli (Przybyla & Byrne, 1984). This raises the interesting possibility that visual stimuli have a particular importance in the male, which is relatively independent of information processing, involving perhaps more direct links between the visual cortex and the hypothalamus.

Interestingly, when men who experience problems with their sexual response (e.g., erectile dysfunction of a psychogenic kind) are compared with "normal" men, distracting cues are less disruptive or may even enhance their response to erotic stimuli, presumably because in their usual situation, their concern about sexual failure is a more powerful form of distraction whose negative effects, including inhibiting or otherwise negative emotional responses, may be reduced by distracting stimuli that have no sexual connotations.

Erotic imagery or fantasy, while of undoubted relevance, does not fit easily into this scheme of things. Variability in the importance of imagery is partly a function of its general use. Whereas "thinking about imaginary situations", or "cognitive rehearsal", is universal, we vary considerably in the extent to which we produce images, either visual or auditory, or even tactile. If such images are more powerful in eliciting a sexual arousal response than simple cognitive rehearsal, their use could account for much of the individual variability in sexual arousability and sexual interest. Furthermore, an erotic image needs to be seen *both as a stimulus and a response*; it can occur as a manifestation of sexual arousal. The hypogonadal man, as a consequence, produces less in the way of erotic imagery.

Mood and emotional states

It has been widely assumed that anxiety or fear is incompatible with sexual response, and the principal theoretical explanations for sexual dysfunction, both psychoanalytic and behavioural, have emphasized the central role played by anxiety. Similarly, it is often assumed that it is difficult to be angry and sexually aroused at the same time. Such negative effects of anxiety or anger on sexual response were attributed to non-specific activation of the sympathetic nervous system in the periphery, leading to inhibition of erection, and so on. There is now little reason to support this view: if sympathetic activation does have an adverse effect, it is by direct and specific inhibition of sexual response, and not as part of generalized sympathetic activation.

Experimental manipulation of emotional states has shown these earlier assumptions to be oversimplifications. In many subjects, particularly those without obvious sexual problems, the induction of any form of arousal, even those with qualities of anxiety or anger, can increase the likelihood of a sexual response to a sexual stimulus (Cranston-Cuebas & Barlow, 1990). On the other hand, situations inducing anxiety or anger may act as distractors, or, if anxiety (or threat) is perceived as related to the sexual stimulus, this may lead to inhibition of sexual response. What is therefore apparent is that neither anxiety nor anger per se are incompatible with sexual response. Their significance in a sexual situation, depend on their origins and their perceived meaning to the subject (Bancroft, 1989).

There has been much less investigation of the relationship between depressed mood and sexual response, perhaps because depression is more difficult to invoke experimentally. The link between mood and sexuality has already been discussed in relation to the menstrual cycle. It is not surprising to find that, in most circumstances, feelings of depression and sexual arousal do not go together. This reflects the negative valence that the mood imparts both to the situation and to the subject's feeling of self-worth. It also reflects the state of inertia rather than arousal that typically characterizes depression. It is, however, possible that biochemical changes associated with depression can have adverse effects on sexual arousability. This is suggested by the impairment of spontaneous sleep erections in states of depression, and their recovery when the depression remits (Thase et al., 1987), together with a common link between the onset of loss of sexual interest and a depressive illness (Schreiner-Engel & Schiavi, 1986).

Social influences and "scripts"

The meaning we attribute to a physiological state will influence reaction to it, and, because of the effects of feedback, how that state evolves. There is an important sex difference in this respect: boys have a physiological signal of sexual response, penile erection, which is not only obvious but also readily

71

labelled as sexual. Once that labelling has occurred, the boy has a ready method of assigning sexual significance to experiences or situations. Not only are girls provided with much less in the way of labels for their genitalia, when they respond physiologically, but also the changes are also less obvious and the attribution of sexual meaning to them less likely. The fact that most girls are older than boys when they recognize their genital responses as sexual may partially explain why social factors appear to have greater influence on the emerging sexuality of adolescent girls than of boys (Udry, Talbert, & Morris, 1986).

The sources of socially derived meanings or "scripts" for sexual behaviour are obviously highly complex (Gagnon & Simon, 1973) and can be considered only in outline in this chapter. At the individual level, the most immediate sources are the family and peer group. These, in turn, will reflect not only cultural patterns, but also religious and socio-economic factors within cultures. Anthropological evidence clearly indicates how such scripts vary across cultures, with some cultures being predominantly "sex positive" and others "sex negative" (Ford & Beach, 1952). The explanations for these cultural contrasts are of considerable interest. Attempts to understand the social evolution of such varied cultural patterns have emphasized the levels of sexual stratification (i.e., the extent to which one gender, usually the male, exerts the power in the social system) and sexual segregation (i.e., the extent to which males and females spend most of their time apart). These in turn reflect the type of social adaptation to the environment, and in particular whether social structure has evolved to the point when property and its inheritance becomes an important issue (Hotvedt, 1990). Thus in hunter-gatherer societies, now virtually extinct, small social groups moved through the environment to where food was available. For them, not only was property of little consequence, but also the patterns of male–female relationships were relatively egalitarian, and attitudes to sexuality relatively positive. This pattern was possibly facilitated by long periods of adolescent infertility, allowing the exploration of sexual relationships before the limitations of child-rearing intervened. As social systems became more settled and more complex, first with pastoral societies, gathering herds of livestock, and later agricultural societies, with the possession of land by a minority and the development of structured social hierarchies, the relevance of sexual stratification and segregation increased, with those of affluence having a particular need to protect the transfer of property by controlling paternity. We can do little but speculate about these very early origins. In more recent historical times, we see strong evidence of striking regional contrasts. Thus, the sexual norms of early Mediterranean societies were dominated by the importance of virginity. Sexual taboos were aimed at avoiding cuckoldry and ensuring that the husband, usually much older than his wife, was the father of any off-spring. In contrast, the northern European tradition, possibly derived from "hunter-gatherer" types of fishing communities, emphasized fertility before marriage, with the "bundling" pattern of courtship, in which the couple paired off and progressed towards sexual intercourse, with marriage following pregnancy (Bancroft, 1989). The socio-political significance of these two contrasting systems is profound, with the northern European pattern more consistent with egalitarian male–female relationships and a single standard of sexual morality. The picture was further complicated by the impact of the Industrial Revolution, its dispersive effect on the extended family, the new opportunities for sexual exploitation of working-class women and the reinforcement of a "double standard" of sexual morality (Schmidt, 1977; Shorter, 1975). Nevertheless, these contrasting patterns are still evident today, in both Europe and the New World.

In more recent times, we have evidence of substantial changes in the pattern of premarital sexual behaviour from the mid-1960s. This was mainly manifested as a narrowing of the differences in sexual experience of adolescent boys and girls, reflecting a weakening of the "double standard" and increase in the ability of girls to enjoy their emerging sexuality (Clement, Schmidt, & Kruse, 1984). Such changes can be explained only in terms of changing social attitudes and "scripts", although the availability of modern methods of fertility control may have aided the process. The contrast between the exceptionally high levels of teenage pregnancy in United States and low levels in European countries such as Sweden and The Netherlands, and the associated contrast in attitudes to sex education and provision of contraceptive advice, is further evidence of the impact of social factors on the pattern of sexual behaviour (Jones et al., 1986).

CONCLUSIONS

We can now consider how these various factors interact to shape the sexuality of our "man" and "woman".

The man's level of sexual interest or desire will be a function of his neurophysiological state of arousal, his awareness of his arousal responses and the meanings he attributes to them, his rehearsal of the sexual "scripts" he has acquired by thoughts and internal images, and his mood. The origins of these components will include genetic and hormonal influences, the effects of learning, and the nature of his relationship with his social group.

His likelihood of expressing such interest as sexual behaviour will depend on his opportunities for action and his ability to enact the scripts appropriately. The likelihood of his repeating the behaviour will depend on its success in meeting his emotional needs at the time, whether it generates positive or negative emotional reactions, and whether it conforms to the norms of the social group that most influences him.

The sexuality of the woman can be understood in basically similar terms. There are potentially important differences in sexual physiology, particularly in relation to the "refractory period". Also, as there may be less emphasis on genital response in her early sexual development, and more emphasis on scripts in which relationships dominate, her constitutional capacity for sexual arousal will be relatively less important than her psychological susceptibility to interpersonal and social pressures. This may explain why, in general, the role of hormones in the sexuality of our woman is less clear than it is with our man.

FURTHER READING

Bancroft, J. (1989). *Human sexuality and its problems* (2nd edn). Edinburgh: Churchill Livingstone.

Ford, C. S., & Beach, F. A. (1952). *Patterns of sexual behaviour*. London: Eyre & Spottiswoode.

Gagnon, J., & Simon, W. (1973). *Sexual conduct: The social sources of human sexuality*. Chicago, IL: Aldine.

Kinsey, A. C., Pomeroy, W. B., Martin, C. F., & Gebhard, P. H. (1953). *Sexual behavior in the human female*. Philadelphia, PA: Saunders.

Masters, W. H., & Johnson, V. E. (1966). *Human sexual response*. Boston, MA: Little, Brown.

REFERENCES

Bancroft, J. (1988). Reproductive hormones and male sexual function. In J. M. A. Sitsen (Ed.) *Handbook of sexology: The pharmacology and endocrinology of sexual function* (vol. 6, pp. 297–315). Amsterdam: Elsevier.

Bancroft, J. (1989). *Human sexuality and its problems* (2nd edn). Edinburgh: Churchill Livingstone.

Beach, F. A. (1976). Sexual attractivity, proceptivity, and receptivity in female mammals. *Hormones and Behavior, 7*, 105–138.

Brownmiller, S. (1975). *Against our will! Men, women and rape*. New York: Simon & Schuster.

Clement, U., Schmidt, G., & Kruse, M. (1984). Changes in sex differences in sexual behaviour: A replication of a study of West German students (1966–1981). *Archives of Sexual Behavior, 13*, 99–120.

Cranston-Cuebas, M. A., & Barlow, D. H. (1990). Cognitive and affective contributions to sexual functioning. *Annual Review of Sex Research, 1*, 119–162.

Darwin, C. (1871). *The descent of man and selection in relation to sex*. London: John Murray.

Davenport-Hines, R. (1990). *Sex, death and punishment*. London: Collins.

Dekker, J., & Everaerd, W. (1988). Attentional effects on sexual arousal. *Psychophysiology, 25*, 45–54.

Dixson, A. F. (1983). The hormonal control of sexual behaviour in primates. *Oxford Reviews of Reproductive Biology, 5*, 131–219.

Everitt, B. J., & Bancroft, J. (1991). Of rats and men: The comparative approach to male sexuality. *Annual Review of Sex Research, 2*, 77–117.

Ford, C. S., & Beach, F. A. (1952). *Patterns of sexual behaviour*. London: Eyre & Spottiswoode.

Gagnon, J., & Simon, W. (1973). *Sexual conduct: The social sources of human sexuality*. Chicago, IL: Aldine.

Geer, J. H., & O'Donohue, W. T. (Eds) (1987). *Theories of human sexuality*. New York: Plenum.

Hart, B. L., & Leedy, M. G. (1985). Neurological bases of male sexual behavior: A comparative analysis. In N. Adler, R. W. Goy, & D. W. Pfaff (Eds) *Handbook of behavioral neurobiology* (vol. 7, pp. 373–422). New York: Plenum.

Hedricks, C., Piccinino, L. J., Udry, J. R., & Chimbia, T. H. (1987). Peak coital rate coincides with onset of luteinizing hormone surge. *Fertility and Sterility*, *48*, 234–238.

Hotvedt, M. E. (1990). Emerging and submerging adolescent sexuality: Culture and sexual orientation. In J. Bancroft & J. M. Reinisch (Eds) *Adolescence and puberty* (pp. 157–172). New York: Oxford University Press.

Jones, E. F., Forrest, J. D., Goldman, N., Henshaw, S. K., Lincoln, R., Rossoff, J. I., Westoff, C. F., & Wul, D. (1986). *Teenage pregnancy in industrialized countries*. New Haven, CT: Yale University Press.

Larsson, K. (1978). Experiential factors in the development of sexual behaviour. In J. Hutchison (Ed.) *Biological determinants of sexual behaviour* (pp. 55–86). Chichester: Wiley.

Money, J., & Ehrhardt, A. A. (1972). *Man and woman, boy and girl: Differentiation and dimorphism of gender identity from conception to maturity*. Baltimore, MD: Johns Hopkins University Press.

Perper, T. (1985). *Sex signals: The biology of love*. New York: Institute for Scientific Information Press.

Przybyla, D. P., & Byrne, D. (1984). The mediating role of cognitive processes in self-reported sexual arousal. *Journal of Research in Personality*, *18*, 54–63.

Sanders, D., Warner, P., Backström, T., & Bancroft, J. (1983). Mood, sexuality, hormones and the menstrual cycle: I. Changes in mood and physical state: Description of subjects and method. *Psychosomatic Medicine*, *45*, 487–501.

Schmidt, G. (1977). Introduction, sociohistorical perspectives. In J. Money & H. Musaph (Eds) *Handbook of sexology* (pp. 269–282). Amsterdam: Excerpta Medica.

Schreiner-Engel, P., & Schiavi, R. C. (1986). Lifetime psychopathology in individuals with low sexual desire. *Psychosomatic Medicine*, *43*, 199–214.

Sherwin, B. B. (1991). The psychoendocrinology of aging and female sexuality. *Annual Review of Sex Research*, *2*, 181–198.

Short, R. V. (1981). Sexual selection in man and the Great Apes. In C. E. Graham (Ed.) *Reproductive biology of the Great Apes* (pp. 319–341). London: Academic Press.

Shorter, E. (1975). *The making of the modern family*. New York: Basic Books.

Thase, M. E., Reynolds, C. F., Glanz, L. M., Jennings, J. R., Sewitch, D. E., Kupfer, D. J., & Frank, E. (1987). Nocturnal penile tumescence in depressed men. *American Journal of Psychiatry*, *144*, 89–92.

Tutin, C. E. G. (1980). Reproductive behaviour of wild chimpanzees in the Gombe National Park, Tanzania. In R. V. Short & B. J. Weir (Eds) *The Great Apes of Africa. Journal of Reproduction and Fertility*. suppl. 28, 43–57.

Udry, J. R., Billy, J. O. G., Morris, N. M., Groff, T. R., & Raj, M. H. (1985). Serum androgenic hormones motivate sexual behavior in adolescent boys. *Fertility and Sterility*, *43*, 90–94.

Udry, J. R., Talbert, L. M., & Morris, N. M. (1986). Biosocial foundations for adolescent female sexuality. *Demography*, *23*, 217–229.

5

STRESS AND COPING

Robert J. Gatchel
University of Texas Southwestern Medical Center, USA

<table>
<tr><td>Early conceptualizations of stress</td><td>Cataclysmic events</td></tr>
<tr><td></td><td>Personal stressors</td></tr>
<tr><td>Walter Cannon</td><td>Background stressors</td></tr>
<tr><td>Hans Selye</td><td>Appraisal of stress</td></tr>
<tr><td>John Mason</td><td>Coping behaviour</td></tr>
<tr><td>Marianne Frankenhaeuser</td><td>Stress, coping, and health</td></tr>
<tr><td>Psychological stress</td><td>Further reading</td></tr>
<tr><td>Types of stressors</td><td>References</td></tr>
</table>

The term *stress* has become part of the lay vernacular, and is widely used as a ready explanation for a number of problems from health complaints to work "burnout" and job dissatisfaction. Moreover, from a scientific point of view, there has been a great deal of research conducted that has demonstrated a relationship between stress and these mental and physical health problems. In these contexts, the term stress is often viewed as a well-delineated construct which has been carefully defined and is quite specific in its effects. However, in this chapter, it will be highlighted how the construct of stress is far from specific, and why there is quite a bit of debate concerning its precise definition.

A major problem associated with defining and measuring stress is that, rather than being an actual entity or "thing", stress is a construct which is inferred in order to account for some form of behaviour. Stress is usually viewed as a mediator, that is, an unobservable inferred construct which is hypothesized to account for a certain observable behaviour such as health or illness differences between individuals. Of course, if one uses a construct to explain some form of behaviour, it is essential that one develops a precise operational definition and employs objective and quantifiable behavioural referents as measures of the construct. As will be seen, this attempt at a precise operational definition is no easy task. Stress is a broad process that involves complex biochemical, physiological, behavioural, and psychological dimensions, many of which are directly or indirectly related to health. At the outset, a rather broad definition of stress will be used: stress is the process by which environmental events threaten or challenge an organism's well-being and by which that organism responds to this threat (Gatchel, Baum, & Krantz, 1989). The environmental events that cause stress are called *stressors*. When such stressors occur, a complex physiological and psychological response mechanism is evoked. When these stressors are intense or become chronic, there are often negative health consequences or outcomes that are produced by them.

EARLY CONCEPTUALIZATIONS OF STRESS

The ancient Greek physician, Hippocrates (*c*.460–*c*.370 BC), who initially proposed that bodily fluids or humours were responsible for certain personality or temperament types, as well as for physical and mental illness, also highlighted the potential negative impact of stress. In his writings, Hippocrates separated suffering caused by disease (*pathos*) from the toil involved in resisting and fighting it (*ponos*). Thus, he suggested a stress-like feature of illness – the energy and wear caused by attempts to combat disease. Since that time, there have been similar notions appearing in the literature (Selye, 1956).

Walter Cannon

It was not until the beginning of the twentieth century, however, that the concept of stress became more scientifically formalized through the work of the physiologist Walter Cannon. Cannon was among the first to actually use the term *stress*, and he clearly indicated that both physiological and psychological components were important. In his physiological studies, he used the term "great emotional stress" to describe a powerful psychophysiological response process that appeared to influence emotion in animals (Cannon, 1928, 1929). His studies clearly demonstrated that emotional stressors such as pain, fear, and rage could cause significant changes in physiological functioning. Cannon pointed out the important "emergency function" of the catecholamines, epinephrine (adrenalin) and norepinephrine (noradrenalin). He suggested that epinephrine played an important role in adaptation by arousing the organism and thereby enabling it to respond more rapidly to danger. Thus, when extremely frightened or enraged, the organism may experience an arousal that may be uncomfortable, but which readies it to act against the stimulus that frightens or angers it.

Initially, these stress-related increases in catecholamines produced by sympathetic nervous system activation, or the "fight or flight" model derivable from Cannon's work, may facilitate adaptive behaviour. This arousal was seen as quite adaptive in helping to increase the ability to resist or enhance the ability to flee the threatening situation. Indeed, some studies have demonstrated superior performance on certain tasks when subjects are injected with epinephrine (Frankenhaeuser, Jarpe, & Mattell, 1961), and also among individuals who produce greater levels of catecholamines in the face of challenge (see Frankenhaeuser, 1971). However, it should also be pointed out that such arousal has been found to be associated with impaired performance on complex tasks (see Evans, 1978).

In Cannon's later writings (Cannon, 1935), stress is clearly seen in terms of both physiological as well as emotional or psychological responses to dangers in the environment. Although stress is seen as an important aid in survival since it mobilizes the organism to take some important action, Cannon also saw it as possibly causing a significant disruption of emotional and physiological stability or homeostasis. He described *critical stress levels* as stress or dangers that affect an organism to such a degree as to disrupt homeostasis or equilibrium which can cause disruption of physiological functioning. Aside from the wear and tear on our bodies generated by repeated or prolonged stress, a variety of negative outcomes is likely to occur when stress does not abate or when there is repeated exposure to stress. Among these consequences are decrements in the ability to cope with subsequent stressors, after-effects, and, in certain cases, physiological dysfunction, tissue damage, or even death (Gatchel et al., 1989).

It should also be noted that Cannon documented the importance of neuroendocrine system responses in the stress response. The "stress hormones" epinephrine and norepinephrine are now often used in research investigations of the stress process: this is an important system operative in the physiological stress response. Stimulation of the sympathetic nervous system causes the adrenal medulla to secrete large amounts of catecholamines, which are neurotransmitter hormones that increase cardiovascular activity, produce vasoconstriction, inhibit gastro-intestinal activity, and increase a number of other bodily functions. In a second major system involved in the stress response process, the pituitary gland secretes the hormone *adrenocorticotropic hormone* (ACTH) that stimulates the adrenal cortex to produce corticosteroids, particularly cortisol. Cortisol affects carbohydrate metabolism and is an anti-inflammatory agent (see Figure 1).

Hans Selye

The early physiological research on emotional stress by Cannon basically laid dormant for many years until Hans Selye's investigations of stress appeared in the literature (Selye, 1956). This research by Selye popularized the notion

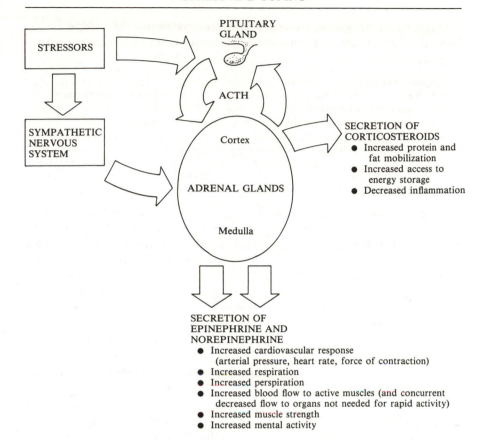

Figure 1 Illustration of the stress-related activities of the adrenal glands

of stress and brought it to the attention of scientists in many different disciplines. As is now well known, Selye's work on stress began quite accidentally in his investigation of sex hormones. Selye found that injections into rats of extracts of ovary tissue produced an unexplainable triad of responses: (1) an enlargement of the adrenal glands which secrete catecholamines and corticosteroids, (2) shrinkage of the thymus gland, and (3) bleeding ulcers. Stimulated by these puzzling findings, Selye subsequently found that extracts of other organs caused the same triad of responses, and that substances not derived from bodily tissue could also cause these responses. He eventually found this same "non-specific" triad of responses to be characteristic of such disparate stimuli as injection of insulin, application of cold or heat, exposure to X-rays, exercise, and so on. His studies clearly showed that each time an alien or aversive stressor agent was applied, changes in the adrenal and thymus glands and the development of ulcers in the acid sensitive stomach lining were observed. This triad of responses was called *non-specific* because it appeared to be caused by *any* noxious or aversive event. Selye (1956) illustrated this notion of a non-specific stress response by comparing it to a burglary:

> Suppose that all possible accesses to a bank building are connected with a police station by an elaborate burglar-alarm system. When a burglar enters the bank, no matter what his personal characteristics are — whether he is small or tall, lean or stout — and no matter which door or window he opens to enter, he will set off the same alarm. The primary change is therefore non-specifically induced from any-where by anyone. The pattern of resulting secondary change, on the other hand, is highly specific. It is always in a certain police station that the burglar alarm will ring and policemen will then rush to the bank along a specified route according to a predetermined plan to prevent robbery. (p. 58)

Thus, a consistent triad of responses is non-specifically induced. In using this concept of non-specific response, Selye then went on to define the stress syndrome as all of the non-specifically induced changes that were produced by a noxious agent. Stress itself was considered a specific state that was the "common denominator of all adaptive reactions in the body". Exposure to a stressor, such as injection of a pathogen, created a response pattern involving, among other things, the original triad of physiological responses.

Selye also introduced the concept of the *General Adaptation Syndrome* (GAS). According to Selye, the GAS consists of three distinct stages of responding (Figure 2). In the first stage, termed the *alarm reaction*, the organism becomes aware of the stressor, or the presence of noxious stimulation. The organism prepares to resist the stressor by mobilizing and activating physiological functioning (e.g., increasing adrenal activity, as well as cardiovascular and respiratory functions, as a means of increasing the body's readiness to respond). The second stage, called the *stage of resistance*, refers to that period when the physiological reserves are ready and circulating levels of corticosteroids have increased. Various coping mechanisms are employed in order to achieve suitable adaptation. During this stage, there is a relatively

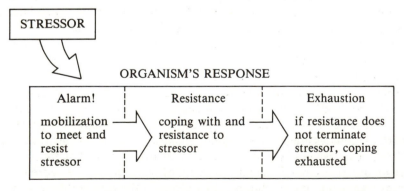

Figure 2   The three stages of Selye's General Adaptation Syndrome

constant resistance to this stressor, but this may be accompanied by a decrease in resistance to other stimuli. When these reactions are repeated many times, or when they are prolonged because of recurring problems, the organism may be placed at risk for irreversible physiological damage. Selye believes that this is the result of the third stage of the GAS, which he refers to as the *exhaustion stage*. During this stage, adaptive reserves are depleted by long-term or repeated conflict with stressors, and resistance is then no longer possible. The result of this exhaustion is likely to be the onset of *diseases of adaptation*. Such illnesses as kidney disease, arthritis, and cardiovascular disease can occur. For example, cardiovascular damage and arthritis may be linked to prolonged elevated levels of catecholamines (Ross & Glomset, 1976). Likewise, high concentrations of inflammatory corticosteroids may be precursors to the onset of arthritis. Also, there is evidence that suggests that prolonged stress can affect immunity (Gatchel et al., 1989). Thus, like Cannon, Selye emphasizes that negative physiological consequences result from prolonged exposure to stressors.

John Mason

Research on the importance of the GAS and how it might be associated with significant health problems caught the attention of the scientific and medical community because of its obvious theoretical and clinical implications. Attention and further development of stress theory increased following the popularization of Selye's work. Moreover, like what happens often in science, criticism of Selye's work also began to appear. One such criticism was the fact that his notion of non-specificity appeared to rule out the possible importance of psychological mechanisms in determining response to a stressor (Mason, 1975). For example, if the same triad of responses were produced regardless of the type of stressor, how might you account for potential individual differences in appraisal and subsequent reaction to the same stressor? Researchers such as John Mason suggested that the process of *psychological appraisal* was very important in determining the type of response produced by a stressor. For example, Mason suggested that stress is neither non-specific nor unitary and that psychological awareness or appraisal of noxious events is an important component necessary for stress to occur. He reported that different patterns of epinephrine, norepinephrine, and corticosteroid secretion were associated with stressors varying in degree of uncertainty or anger and fear elicitation. These are all stressors, but they have different emotional consequences. According to Mason, psychological distress precedes adrenal-pituitary response and may be necessary for physiological reaction to occur.

Mason states that there may be circumstances in which the non-specific stress response of Selye occurs without any psychological input, but the best evidence suggests that awareness of a noxious condition and attempts to deal with it are very crucial in this process. Mason indicates that this awareness need not be conscious in the common use of the term because of the body's ability to attack foreign substances without conscious awareness of the individual. Mason's own work has also demonstrated that physical stressors, such as application of heat, do not elicit adrenal activity when psychological factors involved in the perception and sensation of the stressor are eliminated (see Mason, 1975). Another study reported by Mason compared two groups of dying patients, one composed of people who remained in a coma until they died and the other made up of patients who remained conscious until they passed away. After death, autopsy indicated that the conscious group showed symptoms of stress, such as enlarged adrenal glands, while those who were not conscious showed no such symptoms (Symington, Currie, Curran, & Davidson, 1955).

In fairness to Selye, it should be noted that the notion of psychological appraisal in the stress process can be integrated in the Selye model if one assumes that the non-specific nature of stress is limited to the organism's initial response to a stressor during the alarm stage. If the alarm stage response alone is seen as non-specific, then psychological appraisal or interpretation may still affect subsequent responses during the resistance and exhaustion stages. Thus, one can modify Selye's original model to incorporate some of the more recent research documenting the importance of psychological appraisal and coping mechanisms on the stress response.

Marianne Frankenhaeuser

The work of Marianne Frankenhaeuser and her fellow Swedish colleagues has clearly revealed the strong psychological component involved in the stress response. For example, she has demonstrated that epinephrine and norepinephrine levels can significantly affect the emotional and cognitive functioning in subjects, and that they are secreted in response to purely psychological events (Frankenhaeuser, 1972). In one such study, increases in levels of epinephrine and norepinephrine were associated with decreasing amounts of control over electric shock (Frankenhaeuser & Rissler, 1970). In another study, both understimulation (not having enough to do) and overstimulation (having too much to do) were associated with rises in epinephrine and norepinephrine levels (Frankenhaeuser, Nordheden, Myrsten, & Post, 1971).

In another interesting study, Patkai (1971) demonstrated that increased output of the "stress hormones" epinephrine and norepinephrine were associated not only with noxious or aversive events but also with pleasant but uncontrollable events. In this study, subjects participated in four sessions. During one session, they played a game of chance (a modified bingo game that was generally regarded as being pleasant). In another session, they viewed gruesome surgery films; and in a third session, unpleasant and tedious tasks were performed. Subjects also spent one session in "neutral inactivity" in order to provide a baseline or control for their other experiences. It was found that epinephrine secretion was highest in the pleasant but uncontrollable setting (playing a game), next highest in the less pleasant conditions (tedious task session, film session), and lowest in the inactivity session. Thus, both pleasant and unpleasant events evoke biochemical symptoms of stress (see Figure 3).

This above work is important because it demonstrates the pervasive role that psychological factors can play in eliciting a primary physiological symptom of stress (epinephrine and norepinephrine secretion). This physiological

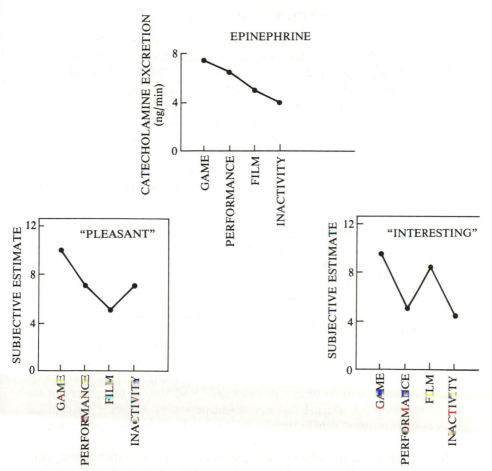

Figure 3 Mean epinephrine levels and ratings of pleasantness for the bingo game (pleasant condition), task and film (less pleasant conditions), and inactivity sessions. Note that higher levels of epinephrine were associated with pleasant and unpleasant events

Source: Patkai, 1971

response, in turn, is associated with psychological responses such as emotionality and cognitive ability. It also suggests a kind of non-specific specificity not unlike Selye's. The same bodily response — secretion of epinephrine and norepinephrine — seems to occur in the face of a wide range of psychological events. Included in a list of stressors that elicit this response are urban commuting, job dissatisfaction, loss of control, conflict, taking examinations, noise, anticipation of an aversive event, and boredom (see Collins & Frankenhaeuser, 1978; Lundberg & Frankenhaeuser, 1976). However, psychological processes can affect the degree or magnitude of this response.

PSYCHOLOGICAL STRESS

This early research on stress clearly documented the importance of biological bases of the stress process. The more recent research has started to focus on the psychological dimension of the stress concept. This has attracted a great deal of interest in the psychological community because, if psychological factors are demonstrated to actually alter bodily function in ways that might facilitate illness, an important link between psychology and health will have been revealed. Indeed, the relationship between the mind and the body has long been a controversial topic among philosophers, physiologists, and psychologists. The Greek physician Hippocrates proposed one of the earliest temperamental theories of personality and suggested that various bodily fluids or humours were associated with specific personality attributes or temperaments. This view of the interrelationship between mind and body, however, lost favour in the seventeenth century with the advent of physical medicine during the Renaissance and the belief that it was unscientific to view that the mind influenced the body. The understanding of the mind and soul was relegated to the areas of religion and philosophy, while the understanding of the body was considered to be in the separate realm of physical medicine. This perpetuated the dualistic viewpoint that mind and body functioned separately and independently. This dualistic viewpoint was further formalized and consolidated by the French philosopher René Descartes, with his Cartesian dualism of mind and body becoming the pre-eminent philosophical basis of medicine. The discovery in the nineteenth century that micro-organisms caused certain diseases produced further acceptance of the dualistic viewpoint. During this new scientific era of medicine, mechanical laws or physiological principles became the only permissible explanations of disease.

Strict dualism mellowed somewhat during the mid-nineteenth century, primarily because of the work of the prominent French physician Claude Bernard, who began to emphasize the contributions of psychological factors to physical ailments. Subsequently, Sigmund Freud was very influential in stressing the interaction of psychological and physical factors in various disorders. Though emphasis was still placed on the body, micro-organisms, and biological determinants of illness, gradually we were becoming more aware of other sources of influence.

The research on stress has renewed the interest in the significant influence of psychological factors in health and illness. The contemporary researcher who has been most responsible for the delineation of the importance of psychological factors in the stress process is Richard Lazarus (1966). By pointing out that stressors can be psychological, Lazarus made the study of stress much more complex and challenging. This is because another level of influence is added to this research area. That is to say, like other aspects of behaviour, psychological stress cannot be measured directly. Instead, it must be inferred from responses or defined in terms of the situations in which it arises.

In dealing with a construct such as stress, it is best to define it operationally as a complex of responses consisting of three broad components of behaviour: (1) subjective or self-report (i.e., asking people how they feel); (2) overt motor behaviours measured by observing performance on certain tasks; and (3) physiological arousal involving primarily the sympathetic branch of the autonomic nervous system, and measuring responses such as epinephrine and norepinephrine levels. What makes the study and measurement of the stress response so difficult is that one cannot always assume that these three broad behaviour component measures will be highly correlated to one another. An individual may verbally report that he or she does not feel "stressed" but yet display increased catecholamine levels and be observed performing poorly on a task requiring concentration. Obviously, it is important to assess all three components of behaviour in specific situations whenever possible, with the expectation that there may be complex interactions among components that may differ from one type of situation to the next.

Indeed, it is useful to group or label stressors in terms of where they occur, what they entail, or their characteristics. As a result, we can discuss occupational stress, urban stress, and the like. The problem is that the impact of the death of a parent, losing a job, or being exposed to crowding is greater than the sum of its effects. What does it mean to experience such stress? This is the real challenge for stress researchers.

TYPES OF STRESSORS

Many external events or situations carry a range of potential problems. Some or all of these problems may be perceived as stressful under certain conditions. In an attempt to categorize types of stressors along a number of dimensions, including how long the stressor persists, the magnitude of response required by the stressor, and the number of people affected, Lazarus and Cohen (1977) have delineated three general categories as stressors: cataclysmic events, personal stressors, and background stressors or daily hassles.

Cataclysmic events

These are stressors that have sudden and powerful impact and are more or less universal in eliciting a stress response. Such events usually require a great deal of effort for effective coping. War, natural disaster, and nuclear accidents are unpredictable and powerful threats that generally affect all of those touched by them. The powerful onset of such cataclysmic events may initially produce a freezing or dazed response by victims. Coping is difficult and may bring no immediate relief. For example, when a severe storm hits an area or when an earthquake occurs in a region, it can be extremely frightening and dangerous to residents, causing severe disruption of people's lives, and causing damage or loss whose impact will not fade for years. However, because the actual event is brief, the severe and threatening aspects of such a stressor dissipate rapidly. Some cataclysmic events, though, cause little physical damage but do not fade quickly. For example, at Love Canal in upstate New York, the discovery of toxic waste and dangers to urban residents was a slow process with little physical destruction. The same was the case for the nuclear accident at Three Mile Island. In these situations, where rebuilding is not what is needed (nothing was actually destroyed), and the damage already done is less important than damage that may yet occur in future years, recovery may be much more difficult. Thus, even within this broad category of cataclysmic events, there may be significant differences in terms of the immediate impact and the long-term consequences on recovery from such a stressor.

Personal stressors

Similar to cataclysmic events, personal stressors are strong and may be unexpected. These types of stressors include events that are powerful enough to challenge adaptive abilities in the same way as the cataclysmic events, but they affect fewer people at any one point in time. This distinction is important to make, since it has been demonstrated that social support has a moderating effect on stress (see Gatchel et al., 1989). In other words, having people around to provide support, help, comparison for emotional and behavioural responses, and other assistance can reduce the negative impact of the stressor. With cataclysmic events, people are able to share distress with others undergoing the same difficulties. However, the second class of stressors (personal stressors) affect fewer people at a time, resulting in fewer people with whom to share the experience. Such events include response to illness, death, or losing one's job.

The death of a parent, for example, is generally an intensely painful loss, and is not always anticipated. The event itself is acute (the death and the immediate period of grief are relatively short) even though, like a disaster, it may leave scars or problems that continue for years. Most typically, the occurrence of the stressor and its immediate aftermath are the most stressful aspects of the experience. Typically, things gradually improve and people may begin to cope with the loss of a loved one by believing that things will continue to improve steadily. However, again, there may be wide individual differences that occur that need to taken into account.

Background stressors

These are persistent, repetitive, and almost routine stressors that are part of one's everyday life. Lazarus and Cohen (1977) have labelled this third group of stressors as daily hassles – stable, repetitive, low-intensity problems encountered daily as part of one's routine. These daily hassles are different from other stressors in many ways. First of all, they are much less powerful than the other two categories of stressors noted above. Cumulatively, over time they may pose threats equally serious, but individually the stressors do not generally pose severe threats. Second, they are chronic. Their impact persists over long periods of time, and the effects of the exposure are gradual. Thus, living in a very noisy neighbourhood may not pose severe threats all at once. That is to say, one exposure to noise is easily coped with and not particularly threatening. However, noise is not usually a one-time event. Rather, it is often repeated and may persist indefinitely. In this context, the notion that things are getting better may not be common: the point at which the worst is over may never occur as things slowly become worse and worse. People can cope with individual episodes of noise even if it is uncontrollable (Glass & Singer, 1972), but the cumulative effects of chronic exposure to noise over time appear to be more severe (Cohen, 1980).

Other chronic stressors include job dissatisfaction, neighbourhood problems, and commuting. In an evaluation of another type of chronic stressor, Thorell, Knox, Svensson, & Waller (1985) reported greater systolic blood pressure elevations among those in high-demand–low-control occupations (such as waiters, drivers, and cooks) than among those in more controllable or less demanding settings. Moreover, Karasek and colleagues have suggested that work stress, which they again operationalized as low control over the work process *and* high work demand, is associated with greater risk for coronary heart disease (Karasek, Theorell, Schwartz, Pieper, & Afredson, 1982). Frankenhaeuser and colleagues have also shown that work stress is associated with coronary risk factors involving catecholamine production, cigarette smoking and sedentary behaviour (e.g., Frankenhaeuser & Johansson, 1982).

Finally, the benefits of social support in order to cope may not be as important with these types of stressors. Even if large numbers of individuals are affected, the duration and magnitude of individual exposure may be too brief to raise the need for affiliation or support. A crowded commute to work is an episodic bout with stress. However, the stress is not severe and can usually be coped with (although it may become increasingly difficult to do so over time). Such an aversive experience probably will not be of sufficient intensity to cause people to band together to provide each other with support and comfort.

In summary, background stressors or daily hassles are chronic, affect large numbers of people *on an individual basis*, and alone do not require a great deal of coping. Yet, the cumulation of stress over a long period of time may result in deceptively severe consequences. Regular and prolonged exposure to low-level stress may require more adaptive responses in the long run than exposure to other stressors. Background stressors generally push an individual's abilities toward their limit. By requiring that people allocate attention and effort to them, they may gradually reduce an individual's ability to cope with subsequent stressors.

APPRAISAL OF STRESS

In his work, Lazarus (1975) emphasizes the role of perception and cognitive appraisal in the stress response process. He argues that unless we perceive the situation as threatening, we will not experience stress. Thus, it could be argued that animals in Selye's experiments may have had to perceive danger before an alarm reaction and the subsequent phases of the GAS could occur. Indeed, in support of this hypothesis, the earlier reviewed study by Symington and colleagues (1955) found that patients who were dying from disease showed no stress response, as measured by adrenal activity, as long as they were unconscious. Lazarus argues that blocking a person's ability to appraise his or her situation as stressful can prevent the onset of the stress response period.

Lazarus has demonstrated the significance of psychological stress over the course of more than twenty years of research. In an initial series of studies conducted during the 1960s, he demonstrated that, by altering the interpretations or appraisals people made while exposed to a stressor, different stress reactions would occur. For example, in one such study, Lazarus, Opton, Nomikos, and Rankin (1965) required that subjects view a gruesome and stressful film depicting woodshop accidents such as a worker cutting off a finger and a worker being killed by a wooden plank driven through his body. Subjects were provided with different narratives when viewing the film. One group of subjects was told that the events had been staged and that no one was really being hurt. Another group was told that events were real but the film would help improve safety in such settings. A third group of subjects was given no explanation. Results demonstrated that both sets of instructions were effective in reducing arousal during the film, relative to the group given no explanation, presumably because such instructions allowed the appraisal of the film in a less threatening manner.

These results were similar to those reported in an earlier study by Lazarus and colleagues (Speisman, Lazarus, Mordkoff, & Davidson, 1964). In this study, subjects were shown a film depicting primitive initiation rites that included rather unpleasant circumcision surgery performed on young adolescents. Subjects viewed the film accompanied by one of three different sound tracts. One group of subjects heard a narration accompanying the film which emphasized the pain, mutilation, and possible disease consequences associated with the circumcision rites (trauma condition); a second group heard a narration in which the pain and consequences were denied and that the participants in the rites were willing and happy because this provided transition from adolescence to adulthood (denial condition); the third group heard a detached description of the rites from an anthropological perspective (intellectualization condition); a fourth group was shown the film with no narration accompanying it. The results of this investigation showed that the psychological stress responses were significantly reduced for subjects in the denial, intellectualization, and no-narration conditions, relative to subjects in the trauma group. Thus, once again, instructions tailored to denial and intellectualization allowed subjects to appraise the situation as less threatening, while instructions given to trauma subjects emphasized those aspects of the film that were more likely to be seen as stressful. Thus, these studies, as well as a number of other studies conducted by Lazarus and his colleagues, provide strong evidence that stress is not well understood in situational terms alone. The films that different groups of subjects saw were the same, and the setting in which they viewed them was similar. However, by altering the interpretations people made while viewing the films (through the narrative or soundtrack manipulation), Lazarus and his colleagues were able to observe different stress reactions.

It should also be pointed out that in some of the studies conducted by Lazarus and colleagues, another source of important variance in stress reactions was also revealed – personality dispositions or tendencies to appraise events in particular ways. For example, in the study of responses to the film depicting circumcision rites, Speisman et al. (1964) found that subjects predisposed to the use of psychological denial as a means of coping with aversive events demonstrated more stress in response to the detached intellectualization soundtrack than to the denial soundtrack. The opposite was true of those subjects who tended to routinely cope by intellectualizing a threat. Differences in appraisal were still found to be responsible for variations in the magnitude of the stress response, but a different source of these differences was demonstrated – situational and personality-based variation in the ways in which a stressor was normally appraised by subjects.

Of course, one must keep in mind the important differences between the type of chronic stressors that were used by investigators such as Selye in demonstrating the biological stress response, and the more acute psychological stressors used by investigators such as Lazarus. There may well be different underlying psychophysiological mechanisms involved in these two types of stress processes. Nevertheless, the significance of the work by Lazarus cannot be overlooked in clearly demonstrating the role that appraisal processes can have on certain stress processes. Thus, we evaluate stressors we encounter, and only those appraised to be threatening evoke the stress response. For example, if one fails an examination, a number of factors will enter into an individual's appraisal of this event. Individuals may consider how much the failure will affect their final grades, whether they feel the failure was their fault or the fault of a bad test, how the failure will affect their self-image, or the extent to which they care about grades or tests. If the failure will not count toward their grade, if they do not care how they do on an exam, or if it does not threaten their self-esteem, the individual will not experience stress. If, on the other hand, the failure is perceived as threatening, stress is more likely to occur.

The role of appraisal mechanisms in the stress process has been widely demonstrated and generally accepted. This has led to important additional research focusing on long-term coping and the kinds of appraisals that can be made to modify the magnitude of stress responses displayed. Such coping processes will be discussed next.

COPING BEHAVIOUR

The above research clearly demonstrates that the impact of any potentially stressful event is significantly influenced by how a person appraises or copes with it. When exposed to a potentially stressful situation, we appraise the setting and make judgements about how threatening it is to us. Lazarus and Launier (1978) have delineated a number of possible appraisals of situations: the evaluation of an event as *irrelevant* (the event in question will not affect the individual); *benign* (the event is positive); and *harmful or threatening interpretations* which may lead to stress. These stressful appraisals may, in turn, be harm or loss assessments involving analyses of damage that already occurred; or threat appraisals concerned with future damages; or challenge appraisals focused on the possibility of overcoming the stressor.

After a situation is judged to be threatening and stressful, secondary appraisals are then made. Now, no longer concerned with assessment of danger, we turn our attention and resources to the dangers or benefits of different modes of coping with the perceived threats. Thus, the perception of danger motivates us to search for coping responses that will reduce this threat.

Gatchel et al. (1989) provide the following example of appraisal of a threat:

> Consider an example of this sequence in a familiar and relatively low-threat event. You feel as if your peers at college exclude you from their activities. When impromptu parties come up, you are the last to find out. People go to the movies without inviting you to go along or go to dinner without waiting for you. You feel

isolated from your fellow students. If you are the kind of person that derives self-esteem or gratification from being part of the "gang," you are more likely to appraise this as threatening and aversive than if you prefer the role of "loner". Let us say you are of the former persuasion. You are upset by this situation and wish to respond. During a second appraisal of the situation, you may consider several approaches. You can do nothing or even withdraw further – the benefits of which are that you do not have to expend energy or risk the rejection that might result from a blatant attempt to join the group. The costs of this coping option are continued isolation and loss of self-esteem. On the other hand, you may make a strong effort to join the group, risking embarrassment and rejection for the possible benefit of being accepted into the group. A third alternative might be to slowly increase your participation in the group. The risks and benefits are similar to those of the second alternative except that the risk of embarrassment is reduced and the period of time before you can feel that you "belong" is greater. You may try to find out why you are being treated as you are so that you understand it better. Finally, you may reinterpret the situation, deciding that you do not want to join the group. By reinterpreting rejection by the group in a positive light, you may reduce loss of self-esteem, but you are still not a member of the group. (pp. 47–48)

Thus, the individual's response to the situation will depend on two kinds of appraisal. First, the individual must interpret the situation and consider its potential threats, harm, or challenge. Is it appraised as threatening or stressful? Second, the individual must consider the response choices. Obviously, evaluation of your choices is based on your interpretation of the situation and nature of the threat you see. By weighing the costs and benefits of these choices, you select an appropriate coping strategy. Thus, the relationship between a stressful event and coping represents a dynamic interplay or process. Coping behaviour can be seen as a series of transactions between an individual who has a certain set of resources, values, and commitments with a particular environment with its own demands and constraints.

Coping behaviour is an important part of the stress response. Moreover, there are literally hundreds of different coping strategies a person might utilize in dealing with a stressful event. For the sake of convenience, these coping strategies have been grouped into five general categories by Cohen and Lazarus (1979):

1 *Direct action responses*, where the individual tries to directly manipulate or alter his or her relationship to the stressful situation. For example, an individual may change the setting, flee, or otherwise remove the physical presence of the stressor.
2 *Information seeking*, in which an individual may seek information about the situation so that he or she can understand it and predict related events. Gathering information about the stressful event may be helpful in use for problem solving or emotional regulation. For example, the individual exposed to chronic commuting stress might seek more information about the commuting situation either to reduce his or her anxiety or to make decisions about alternative possibilities.

3 *Inhibition of action*, which involves doing nothing in a situation. This may be the best course of action in some situations, especially if it is seen as a short-term impact or event.

4 *Intrapsychic or palliative coping*, in which the individual accommodates the stressful situation by reappraising the situation or by altering his or her "internal environment". Taking drugs, drinking alcohol, learning to relax, creating or using psychological defence mechanisms, and engaging in meditation are examples of this type of coping.

5 *Turning to others* for help and emotional support involves mobilizing one's social support network to help with the situation. Thus, an individual who is attempting to cope with a particular problem might try to mobilize support from within the family.

An individual will use a wide variety of different coping strategies in managing a single stressor. The same individual may, for example, engage in intrapsychic coping, turning to others for support, and information seeking at different points in time in coping with the event. Which specific coping behaviour will be used at a particular point in time depends in large part on the nature of the stressor itself and the potential problems that may be present in a particular setting within which the stressful event has arisen.

STRESS, COPING, AND HEALTH

As we have seen in this chapter, stress is a major behavioural/psychological link to illness. Chronic stressors can cause neural and endocrine change that alters the normal functioning of the organism (e.g., change in cardiovascular activity or immune system functioning). This physiological response to stress is also accompanied by behavioural responses. Individuals will respond to stress with a variety of coping mechanisms. Stress and the subsequent behavioural response to it can affect health and facilitate, if not cause, some illnesses. Stress has direct physiological effects on the body, and the cumulative wear and tear on the system caused by recurring stress can eventually cause damage to the system. There is abundant evidence that stress can cause a number of physiological and biochemical changes. There is also a growing literature indicating that some of these changes can be linked directly to illness.

There have thus been attempts to develop stress management techniques in order to help individuals deal with stress and avoid negative psychophysiological consequences. Indeed, health psychologists have paid great attention to developing techniques of stress management that can be taught to large groups of people. This is because stress-related disorders appear to account for as much as $17 billion per year in lost productivity, with some estimates placing the annual cost of stress-related illnesses at $60 billion (Adams, 1978). This has caused increased motivation on the part of businesses and organizations to help their workers identify and cope more effectively with a variety of stressful events that they may experience on the job.

It is beyond the scope of this chapter to review the major components and types of stress management programmes. There is a rapidly growing literature on this topic. It should be noted, though, that these stress management programmes have been developed and utilized extensively with populations that already suffer from a stress-related illness or that are at high risk for a stress-related illness. Thus, individuals with psychophysiological disorders such as essential hypertension, headache, and gastro-intestinal problems have been treated with such techniques (Gatchel et al., 1989). Moreover, stress management techniques have also been developed as a means of modifying type A behaviour which is associated with increased risk of coronary heart disease (e.g., Roskies et al. 1986). Such programmes have been documented to be helpful, and results demonstrating a decrease in physiological symptomatology again point to the close link between stress, behaviour, and illness/health.

In conclusion, stress has been a topic of concern for centuries, and was formalized in the early twentieth century by Cannon. Subsequent scientific study of stress by investigators such as Selye, Mason, Frankenhaeuser, and Lazarus further demonstrated the important physiological and psychological concomitants of the stress process. This research has revealed that behavioural factors and stress are involved in the development of many illnesses, and highlights the important role that psychological factors play in health and illness.

FURTHER READING

Antonovsky, A. (1987). *Unraveling the mystery of health: How people manage stress and stay well*. San Franciso, CA: Jossey-Bass.

Friedman, H. S. (Ed.) (1991). *Hostility, coping and health*. Washington, DC: American Psychological Association.

Gatchel, R. J., Baum, A., & Krantz, D. S. (1989). *An introduction to health psychology*. New York: Random House.

Lazarus, R., & Folkman, S. (1984). *Stress, appraisal and coping*. New York: Springer.

REFERENCES

Adams, J. D. (1978). Improving stress management: Action-research based on intervention. In W. W. Burke (Ed.) *The cutting edge*. La Jolla, CA: University Associates.

Cannon, W. B. (1928). Neural organization for emotional expression. In M. L. Reymert (Ed.) *Feelings and emotions: The Wittenberg symposium*. Worcester, MA: Clark University Press.

Cannon, W. B. (1929). *Bodily changes in pain, hunger, fear and rage*. Boston, MA: Branford.

Cannon, W. B. (1935). Stresses and strains of homeostasis. *American Journal of Medical Science, 189*, 1–14.

Cohen, F., & Lazarus, R. (1979). Coping with the stresses of illness. In G. C. Stone, F. Cohen, & N. E. Ader (Eds) *Health psychology: A handbook.* San Francisco, CA: Jossey-Bass.

Cohen, S. (1980). Aftereffects of stress on human performance and social behavior: A review of research and theory. *Psychological Bulletin, 88*, 82–108.

Collins, A., & Frankenhaeuser, M. (1978). Stress responses in male and female engineering students. *Journal of Human Stress, 4*, 43–48.

Evans, G. W. (1978). Human spatial behavior: The arousal model. In A. Baum & Y. M. Epstein (Eds) *Human response to crowding.* Hillsdale, NJ: Lawrence Erlbaum.

Frankenhaeuser, M. (1971). Behavior and circulating catecholamines. *Brain Research, 31*, 241–262.

Frankenhaeuser, M. (1972). *Biochemical events, stress and adjustments.* Reports from the Psychological Laboratories, University of Stockholm, no. 368.

Frankenhaeuser, M., & Johansson, G. (1982). *Stress at work: Psychobiological and psychosocial aspects.* Paper presented at the 20th International Congress of Applied Psychology, Edinburgh, July.

Frankenhaeuser, M., & Rissler, A. (1970). Effects of punishment on catecholamine release and efficiency of performance. *Psychopharmacologia, 17*, 378–390.

Frankenhaeuser, M., Jarpe, G., & Mattell, G. (1961). Effects of intravenous infusions of adrenaline and noradrenaline on certain psychological and physiological functions. *Acta Physiological Scandinavia, 51*, 175–186.

Frankenhaeuser, M., Nordheden, B., Myrsten, A. L., & Post, B. (1971). Psychophysiological reactions to understimulation and overstimulation. *Acta Psychologia, 35*, 298–308.

Gatchel, R. J., Baum, A., & Krantz, D. S. (1989). *An introduction to health psychology.* New York: Random House.

Glass, D. C., & Singer, J. E. (1972). *Urban stress.* New York: Academic Press.

Karasek, R. A., Theorell, T. G., Schwartz, J., Pieper, C., & Afredsson, L. (1982). Job, psychological factors and coronary heart disease: Swedish prospective findings and U.S. prevalence findings using a new occupational inference method. *Advances in Cardiology, 29*, 62–67.

Lazarus, R. S. (1966). Story telling and the measurement of motivation: The direct versus substitutive controversy. *Journal of Consulting Psychology, 30*, 483–561.

Lazarus, R. S. (1975). A cognitively oriented psychologist looks at biofeedback. *American Psychologist, 30*, 553–561.

Lazarus, R. S., & Cohen, J. B. (1977). Environmental stress. In I. Attman & J. F. Wohlwill (Eds) *Human behavior and the environment: Current theory and research* (vol. 2). New York: Plenum.

Lazarus, R. S., & Launier, R. (1978). Stress-related transactions between person and environment. In L. A. Pervin & M. Lewis (Eds) *Internal and external determinants of behavior.* New York: Plenum.

Lazarus, R. S., Opton, E. M., Jr, Nomikos, M. S., & Rankin, N. O. (1965). The principle of short-circuiting of threat: Further evidence. *Journal of Personality, 33*, 622–635.

Lundberg, U., & Frankenhaeuser, M. (1976). *Adjustment to noise stress.* Reports from the Department of Psychology, University of Stockholm, no. 484.

Mason, J. W. (1975). A historical view of the stress field. *Journal of Human Stress, 1*, 22–36.

Patkai, P. (1971). Catecholamine excretion in pleasant and unpleasant situations. *Acta Psychologica*, *35*, 352–363.

Roskies, E., Seraganian, P., Oseasohn, R., Martin, N., Smilga, C., & Hanley, J. A. (1986). The Montreal Type A intervention project: Major findings. *Health Psychology*, *5*, 45–60.

Ross, R., & Glomset, J. A. (1976). The pathogenesis of artherosclerosis. *New England Journal of Medicine*, *295*, 369–377.

Selye, H. (1956). *The stress of life*. New York: McGraw-Hill.

Speisman, J., Lazarus, R. S., Mordkoff, A., & Davidson, L. (1964). Experimental reduction of stress based on ego defense theory. *Journal of Abnormal and Social Psychology*, *20*, 156–164.

Symington, T., Currie, A. R., Curran, R. S., & Davidson, J. (1955). The reaction of the adrenal cortex in conditions of stress. In *Ciba Foundations Colloquia on Endocrinology* (vol. 8). Boston, MA: Little, Brown.

Theorell, T., Knox, S., Svensson, J., & Waller, D. (1985). Blood pressure variations during a working day at age 28: Effects of different types of work and blood pressure level at age 18. *Journal of Human Stress*, *11*, 36–41.

GLOSSARY

This glossary is confined to a selection of frequently used terms that merit explanation or comment. Its informal definitions are intended as practical guides to meanings and usages. The entries are arranged alphabetically, word by word, and numerals are positioned as though they were spelled out.

acetylcholine one of the neurotransmitter (q.v.) substances that play a part in relaying information between neurons.

ACh a common abbreviation for acetylcholine (q.v.).

achievement motivation *see* need for achievement (achievement motivation).

ACTH *see* adrenocorticotropic hormone (ACTH).

adolescence from the Latin *adolescere*, to grow up, the period of development between puberty and adulthood.

adrenal glands from the Latin *ad*, to, *renes*, kidneys, a pair of endocrine glands (q.v.), situated just above the kidneys, which secrete adrenalin (epinephrine), noradrenalin (norepinephrine) (qq.v.), and other hormones (q.v.) into the bloodstream. *See also* adrenocorticotropic hormone (ACTH).

adrenalin(e) hormone secreted by the adrenal glands (q.v.), causing an increase in blood pressure, release of sugar by the liver, and several other physiological reactions to perceived threat or danger. *See also* endocrine glands, noradrenalin(e).

adrenocorticotropic hormone (ACTH) a hormone secreted by the pituitary gland (q.v.) that stimulates the adrenal gland (q.v.) to secrete corticosteroid hormones such as cortisol (hydrocortisone) into the bloodstream, especially in response to stress or injury.

afferent neurons from the Latin *ad*, to, *ferre*, to carry, neurons (q.v.) that transmit impulses from the sense organs to the central nervous system (CNS) (q.v.). *Cf.* efferent neurons.

alarm reaction the first stage in the general adaptation syndrome (q.v.) according to Hans Selye's three-stage interpretation of an organism's physiological reaction to stress. It is characterized by an initial fall in body temperature and blood pressure, and a subsequent countershock phase during which hormones (q.v.) are secreted into the bloodstream and a biological defensive reaction begins.

amphetamine any of a class of commonly abused drugs including Benzedrine, Dexedrine, and Methedrine that act as central nervous system stimulants, suppress appetite, increase heart-rate and blood pressure, and induce euphoria.

androgens from the Greek *andros*, man, *genes*, born, any of a number of male sex hormones, notably testosterone, secreted by the testes and the adrenal glands in males and in small amounts by the ovaries and the adrenal glands in females, responsible for the development of masculine secondary sexual characteristics.

androgynous from the Greek *andros*, man, *gyne*, woman, having both masculine and feminine qualities.

anorexia nervosa from the Greek *an*, lacking, *orexis*, appetite, an eating disorder, mostly of women, characterized by self-induced weight loss, a morbid fear of fatness which does not diminish as weight decreases, and a disturbance of body image (feeling fat even when emaciated). *Cf.* bulimia nervosa.

antidepressant drugs drugs that influence neurotransmitters (q.v.) in the brain, used in the treatment of mood disorders (q.v.), especially depression (q.v.). The monoamine oxidase inhibitor (MAOI) drugs block the absorption of amines such as dopamine, adrenalin, and noradrenalin (qq.v.), allowing these stimulants to accumulate at the synapses in the brain, the tricyclic antidepressants such as imipramine act by blocking the re-uptake of noradrenalin in particular, thereby similarly increasing its availability, and the selective serotonin re-uptake inhibitor fluoxetine hydrochloride (Prozac) blocks the re-uptake of serotonin (q.v.).

arousal a general term for an organism's state of physiological activation, mediated by the autonomic nervous system (q.v.). *See also* Yerkes-Dodson law.

audience effect *see under* social facilitation.

autonomic nervous system a subdivision of the nervous system (q.v.) that regulates (autonomously) the internal organs and glands. It is divided into the sympathetic nervous system and the parasympathetic nervous system (qq.v.).

axon from the Greek word meaning axis, a process or extending fibre of a neuron (q.v.) which conducts impulses away from the cell body (q.v.) and transmits them to other neurons.

bulimia nervosa from the Greek *bous*, ox, *limos*, hunger, an eating disorder, confined almost exclusively to women, characterized by recurrent episodes of binge eating, usually followed by self-induced vomiting and/or laxative abuse, and a morbid fear of fatness. *Cf.* anorexia nervosa.

catecholamine any member of the group of hormones (q.v.) that are catechol derivatives, especially adrenalin, noradrenalin, and dopamine, (qq.v.), all of which are involved in the functioning of the nervous system (q.v.).

cell body sometimes called the *soma*, the central part of a neuron (q.v.), containing the nucleus and other structures that keep the cell alive.

central nervous system (CNS) in human beings and other vertebrates, the brain and spinal cord.

CNS *see* central nervous system (CNS).

co-action effect *see under* social facilitation.

cognition from the Latin *cognoscere*, to know, attention, thinking, problem-solving, remembering, and all other mental processes that fall under the general heading of information processing.

cortisol *see under* adrenocorticotropic hormone (ACTH).

correlation in statistics, the relationship between two variables such that high scores on one tend to go with high scores on the other or (in the case of negative correlation) such that high scores on one tend to go with low scores on the other. The usual index of correlation, called the product-moment correlation coefficient and symbolized by r, ranges from 1.00 for perfect positive correlation, through zero for uncorrelated variables, to -1.00 for perfect negative correlation.

DA a common abbreviation for dopamine (q.v.).

dendrite from the Greek *dendron*, tree, the collection of branched, threadlike extensions of a neuron (q.v.) that receives impulses, from other neurons or from a receptor and conducts them towards the cell body (q.v.).

depression a sustained negative mood state characterized by sadness, pessimism, a general feeling of despondency, passivity, indecisiveness, suicidal thoughts, sleep disturbances, and other mental and physical symptoms, associated with some mood disorders (q.v.).

dopamine a catecholamine (q.v.); one of the neurotransmitter (q.v.) substances significantly involved in central nervous system functioning. *See also* antidepressant drugs.

efferent neurons from the Latin *e*, from, *ferre*, to carry, neurons that transmit impulses away from the central nervous system (CNS) towards the muscles, glands, etc. *Cf.* afferent neurons.

emotion from the Latin *e*, away, *movere*, to move, any evaluative, affective, intentional, short-term psychological state. *See also* expressive behaviour, James-Lange theory, opponent-process theory of motivation, primary emotions.

endocrine gland any ductless gland, such as the adrenal gland or pituitary gland (qq.v.), that secretes hormones directly into the bloodstream. The endocrine system functions as an elaborate signalling system within the body, alongside the nervous system.

endorphins from the Greek *endon*, within, and morphine, from *Morpheus*, the Greek god of sleep and dreams, any of a class of morphine-like substances occurring naturally in the brain that bind to pain receptors and thus block pain sensations.

epinephrine, norepinephrine from the Greek *epi*, upon, *nephros*, kidney, alternative words for adrenalin and noradrenalin (qq.v.), especially in United States usage. *See also* endocrine gland.

expressive behaviour behaviour, especially facial expressions and other forms of non-verbal behaviour, that expresses emotional states or attitudes. *See also* emotion, primary emotions, non-verbal communication.

factor analysis a statistical technique for analysing the correlations between a large number of variables in order to reduce them to a smaller number of underlying dimensions, called factors, in a manner analogous to the way in which all spectral colours can be reduced to combinations of just three primary colours.

fight or flight mechanism a response to perceived danger or threat in which catecholamines (q.v.) are released into the bloodstream and physiological arousal increases, temporarily increasing the organism's chances of survival, either by staying and fighting or fleeing.

5-hydroxytryptamine (5-HT) another name for serotonin (q.v.).

general adaptation syndrome (GAS) the three-stage biological response of an organism to severe stress according to Hans Selye, comprising the alarm reaction (q.v.), resistance stage, and exhaustion stage.

hippocampus from the Greek *hippos*, horse, *kampos*, sea monster, a structure in the brain, whose cross section has the shape of a sea horse, involved in emotion, motivation, learning, and the establishment of long-term memory (q.v.).

homeostasis from the Greek *homos*, same, *stasis*, stoppage, the maintenance of equilibrium in any physiological or psychological process by automatic compensation for disrupting changes.

hormone from the Greek *horman*, to stir up or urge on, a chemical substance secreted into the bloodstream by an endocrine gland (q.v.) and transported to another part of the body where it exerts a specific effect.

James-Lange theory a theory proposed independently by William James in the United States and Carl Lange in Denmark asserting that bodily changes precede subjective emotional experiences and that it is the perception of these bodily changes that are (or cause) the subjective emotional experiences. *See also* emotion.

limbic system a ring of structures surrounding the brain stem concerned with emotion, hunger, and sex.

mood disorders a group of mental disorders characterized by disturbances of affect or mood, including especially depression (q.v.), bipolar disorder and mania.

motivation the motive forces responsible for the initiation, persistence, direction, and vigour of goal-directed behaviour.

NA a common abbreviation for noradrenalin (q.v.).

NE a common abbreviation for norepinephrine. *See* noradrenalin.

need for achievement (achievement motivation) a social form of motivation (q.v.) involving a competitive drive to meet standards of excellence, traditionally measured with a projective test such as the Thematic Apperception Test (TAT) *Cf.* need for affiliation.

need for affiliation a social form of motivation (q.v.) involving a drive to associate and interact with other people. *Cf.* need for achievement (achievement motivation).

nervous system *see under* autonomic nervous system, central nervous system (CNS), parasympathetic nervous system, sympathetic nervous system.

neuron from the Greek word for nerve, a nerve cell, which is the basic structural and functional unit of the nervous system, consisting of a cell body, axon, and dendrites (qq.v.). *See also* afferent neuron, efferent neuron.

neurophysiology the study of the operation of the nervous system (q.v.).

neuroscience an interdisciplinary field of study concerned with the anatomy, physiology, development, and biochemistry of the nervous system (q.v.), and its effects on behaviour and mental experience.

neurotransmitter a chemical substance such as acetylcholine, dopamine, serotonin, or noradrenalin (qq.v.) by which a neuron (q.v.) communicates with another neuron or with a muscle or gland.

non-verbal communication the collective name for all forms of communication apart from spoken or written language, including the communicative effects of vocal quality, facial expression, postures, and gestures.

noradrenalin one of the catecholamine (q.v.) hormones and an important neurotransmitter (q.v.) in the nervous system, also called norepinephrine, especially in United States usage.

norepinephrine *see* noradrenalin.

oestradiol the most potent of the oestrogen (q.v.) hormones.

oestrogen any of a number of female sex hormones.

opponent-process theory of motivation any of several theories that state that, because of homeostasis (q.v.), any emotion (q.v.) is likely to be followed by its opposite.

parasympathetic nervous system one of the two major divisions of the autonomic nervous system (q.v.); its general function is to conserve metabolic energy. *Cf.* sympathetic nervous system.

peptides chemical substances such as endorphins (q.v.) that regulate various bodily functions and play an important part in the experience of pain.

personality from the Latin *persona*, mask, the sum total of all the behavioural and mental characteristics that distinguish an individual from others.

pituitary gland the master endocrine gland (q.v.), attached by a stalk to the base of the brain, which secretes into the bloodstream hormones affecting bodily growth and the functioning of other endocrine glands. *See also* adrenocorticotropic hormone (ACTH).

primary emotions according to Paul Ekman, the six emotions of happiness, sadness, disgust, fear, anger, and surprise, so-called partly because their associated facial expressions are evidently innate: many appear soon after birth, even in infants born blind and deaf, and have been found to be similar in all cultures that have been studied. *See also* emotion, expressive behaviour, non-verbal communication.

progesterone a female sex hormone that prepares the uterus for the fertilized ovum and maintains pregnancy.

psychology from the Greek *psyche*, mind, *logos*, study, the study of the nature, functions, and phenomena of behaviour and mental experience.

psychoneuroimmunology the study of the interrelationships between mental function, the nervous system, and the immune system.

psychosomatic from the Greek *psyche*, mind *soma*, body, of or relating to disorders thought to be caused or aggravated by psychological factors such as stress.

receptor a sense organ or structure that is sensitive to a specific form of physical energy and that transmits neural information to other parts of the nervous system.

sensory memory a form of memory, necessary for normal vision and hearing, which allows visual images to be stored for about half a second and sounds for up to two seconds. Sensory memory enables television, which presents 30 still images per second, to convey the illusion of a single moving image. It also makes speech intelligible, because without it, by the end of each spoken word the hearer would have forgotten its beginning. *See also* sensory registers. *Cf.* long-term memory, short-term memory.

sensory registers subsystems of sensory memory (q.v.), such as (for vision) the iconic store and (for hearing) the echoic store, generally assumed to exist separately for each sensory modality.

serotonin one of the neurotransmitter (q.v.) substances in the nervous system, also known as 5-hydroxytryptamine or 5-HT.

short-term memory (STM) a memory store, also called working memory, consisting of a central executive, visuo-spatial sketchpad, and articulatory loop that is used for storing small amounts of information for periods of time ranging from a few seconds to a few minutes. It has a severely limited capacity of about seven or eight items of information, such as digits of a telephone number, and the information is rapidly forgotten unless it is refreshed by rehearsal, following which it may eventually be transferred to long-term memory (LTM) (q.v.). *See also* sensory memory.

social facilitation the enhancing effect on behaviour of the mere presence of others, either as passive spectators (audience effect) or as co-actors (co-action effect).

social learning learning that occurs through observation of the behaviour of others, called models, together with imitation, and vicarious learning.

social motivation any form of motivation (q.v.) associated with social behaviour, manifested in such phenomena as need for achievement (achievement motivation), need for affiliation, and social facilitation (qq.v.).

somatoform disorders a class of mental disorders (q.v.) characterized by deterioration of physical functioning without any discernable physiological cause, specifically when there is evidence that the physical symptoms have psychological causes and there is lack of voluntary control over the physical symptoms and indifference to the deterioration of physical functioning.

state-dependent memory memory for information learned in a particular state of consciousness – for example, in a particular emotional state or under the influence of alcohol or drugs – that can be recalled only when in a similar state. Thus material learned in an intoxicated state is sometimes remembered only in a later intoxicated state, and a person in a depressed state may perhaps be more likely to remember unhappy experiences from the past, which might exacerbate the depression and create a vicious circle.

stimulants hormones such as adrenalin, noradrenalin, and dopamine (qq.v.), and drugs such as amphetamines (q.v.), that increase physiological arousal in general and central nervous system (q.v.) activity in particular.

stressor any stimulus, event or state of affairs that causes stress.

subjects from the Latin *sub*, under, *jacere*, to throw, people or other organisms whose behaviour or mental experience is investigated in psychological research.

sympathetic nervous system one of the two major divisions of the autonomic nervous system; it is concerned with general activation, and it mobilizes the body's reaction to stress or perceived danger. *Cf.* parasympathetic nervous system.

testosterone one of the most important of the androgens (q.v.).

Type A behaviour pattern a personality type, possibly associated with an increased risk of coronary heart disease, characterized by an exaggerated sense of urgency, competitiveness, ambition, and hostile aggressiveness when thwarted.

Yerkes-Dodson law a psychological law named after its proposers stating that optimal performance on a variety of tasks occurs at intermediate levels of arousal (q.v.).

INDEX